QUIET TIME

One Year Daily Devotional for Children in Grades 1–2

Quiet Time

One year daily devotional for children in grades 1-2

Published by Word of Life Local Church Ministries
A division of Word of Life Fellowship, Inc.
Joe Jordan - Executive Director
Don Lough - Director
Jack Wyrtzen & Harry Bollback - Founders
Mike Calhoun - VP of Local Church Ministries

USA
P.O. Box 600
Schroon Lake, NY 12870
1-888-932-5827
talk@wol.org

Canada
RR#8/Owen Sound
ON, Canada N4K 5W4
1-800-461-3503 or (519) 376-3516
lcm@wol.ca

Web Address: www.wol.org

Publisher's Acknowledgements
Writers and Contributors: Gretchen Gregory, Jennifer Huntington, Elizabeth Kuhlken, Lisa Reichard
Editor: Lisa Reichard
Curriculum Manager: Don Reichard
Design and layout: Sally Robison

ISBN – 978-1-931235-77-8
Printed in the United States of America

God loves you and wants to spend time with you!

Quiet Time is a special time that you set aside each day to read God's Word to get to know Him better and to learn how He wants you to live. During this time, God speaks to you through His Holy Word, the Bible, and you speak to God through prayer. What an adventure! As a Christian, spending this time everyday is very important for you to grow closer to God.

This Quiet Time will help you have a special time each day with the Lord. This booklet is divided into two sections: *A Personal Prayer Diary* section where you can write prayer requests to remind yourself to pray for people that you care about and things that are happening and the *Quiet Time Activity Pages* where activities are written from the Bible verses for each day of the year to challenge you to understand the truths from God's Word.

All Word of Life Quiet Times use the same Scriptures for the week. This makes it easier for your whole family to discuss the passages together.

Meet the Challenger friends.

Here are some new friends that you will get to know this year.
They will help and encourage you daily as you spend time with God.

A Note to Parents

This Quiet Time is a great opportunity for you to have fun together with your child.
Here are some tips to help your child with the Quiet Time.

- Sit down at a prescribed time each day.
- Gather supplies needed for activities.
- Use the Bible to look up references together.
- Talk through the activity and personal application.

- Encourage your child to use the prayer suggestions in the Pray section and occasionally pray with them.
- Complete the week by documenting how many days were completed and writing an encouraging note.

Your Daily Quiet Time

SUNDAY — Psalm 26:3

"Jump for Joy"

David thought a lot about all the great things God does for us.

When he thought about God, it was hard for him to be quiet.

He just wanted to sing and thank God forever.

Begin the week by reading the cartoon featuring your Challenger Friends. This will give you a hint about what you will learn that week.

Wow! God's love is always with you.

Write or draw one place where God's love will be with you today.

Pray
Thank God that His love is always with you.

Each day, read the Daily Scripture Passage in your Bible.

MONDAY — Psalm 27:1

The Lord is your <u>light</u> and your <u>salvation</u>. The Lord keeps you <u>safe</u>. You don't need to be afraid.

Fill in the answer and complete the crossword puzzle.

Down
1. The Lord is my
_ _ _ _ _ _ _

Across
1. The Lord will keep me
_ _ _ _
2. The Lord is my
_ _ _ _ _

Pray
Ask God to help you when you are afraid.

18

TUESDAY — Psalm 28:7

Trust in God with all your heart. He will help you. Don't forget to thank Him for His help.

Connect the dots and trace the word inside to find out who will help you.

Pray
Thank God for all the ways He helps you.

Complete the activity for the day.

Use the Pray statement to guide you as you pray each day.

Write down your prayer requests in your diary and spend time talking to God in prayer.

6

Things I need for my Quiet Time:

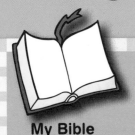
My Bible

My Quiet Time

Crayons or Markers

A Quiet Place

My Personal Prayer Diary

Spending time with God in Prayer

Keeping a Personal Prayer Diary is a great way to remind yourself to pray for specific people and things. It also reminds you to thank God and to tell others when He answers your prayers.

Your prayer time should include praying for friends and family. Especially pray for those who don't know Christ as their Savior.

You should also pray for your Christian friends, your relatives and yourself. Pray that you will grow in your Christian life and become what God wants you to be.

Get to know missionaries who serve the Lord in your area or around the world. Ask them for specific prayer requests. Write these on your prayer pages.

Much of your prayer time should be used thanking and praising God. Tell God that you are thankful for your salvation, parents, home, friends, and answers to prayers. You should praise God for His beautiful creation, His holiness and His greatness.

Some prayer time should include asking God to meet needs such as clothing, food or maybe a job for your dad. Maybe you could ask God to help you be more obedient. You must be careful not to be selfish and ask for things that you want only for you. As you are obedient to God, He will care for your needs.

Daily Prayer Requests

Daily Prayer Requests are those things that you pray for each day. Maybe someone in your family will be traveling one day and you ask God to protect them as they travel. For each request, write the date that you started praying for it and how God answered your prayer.

Name	Date	How My Prayer Was Answered

Daily Prayer Requests

Name	Date	How My Prayer Was Answered

Daily Prayer Requests

Name	Date	How My Prayer Was Answered

SUNDAY—family + friends

Name	Date	How My Prayer Was Answered

MISSIONARIES + CHURCH LEADERS

I THANK GOD FOR...	I PRAISE GOD FOR...

MONDAY–family + friends

Name	Date	How My Prayer Was Answered

MISSIONARIES + CHURCH LEADERS

Name	Date	How My Prayer Was Answered

I THANK GOD FOR...	I PRAISE GOD FOR...

TUESDAY—family + friends

Name	Date	How My Prayer Was Answered

MISSIONARIES + CHURCH LEADERS

I THANK GOD FOR...	I PRAISE GOD FOR...

WEDNESDAY–family + friends

Name	Date	How My Prayer Was Answered

MISSIONARIES + CHURCH LEADERS

Name	Date	How My Prayer Was Answered

I THANK GOD FOR... | I PRAISE GOD FOR...

I THANK GOD FOR...	I PRAISE GOD FOR...

14

THURSDAY—family + friends

Name	Date	How My Prayer Was Answered

MISSIONARIES + CHURCH LEADERS

Name	Date	How My Prayer Was Answered

I THANK GOD FOR...	I PRAISE GOD FOR...

15

FRIDAY—family + friends

Name	Date	How My Prayer Was Answered

MISSIONARIES + CHURCH LEADERS

Name	Date	How My Prayer Was Answered

I THANK GOD FOR... | I PRAISE GOD FOR...

I thank God for...	I praise God for...

SATURDAY–family + friends

Name	Date	How My Prayer Was Answered

MISSIONARIES + CHURCH LEADERS

Name	Date	How My Prayer Was Answered

I THANK GOD FOR...	I PRAISE GOD FOR...

17

"Keep In Touch"

We keep in touch with people we care about by writing letters or email and calling them. How can we keep in touch with God? What would you tell Him?

I thank Him for the good things in my life.

I listen to what God says when I read the Bible.

I talk to God about my problems.

SUNDAY
Psalm 51:9

As you do your quiet time, you will learn more and more about sin, repentance, and salvation through Jesus. Make a promise to do your quiet time every day.

Hide your face from my sins and blot out my iniquity.

Did you know you were born a sinner? Sin is found in each and every one of us. That doesn't make sin okay. God still hates sin, but God gives you hope in Jesus.

> **I pledge to do my quiet time every day.**
>
> _Trevin_
> NAME
>
> _____
> DATE

Pray
Ask God to help you do your quiet time every day.

MONDAY
Psalm 52:9

TUESDAY
Psalm 53:3

David makes a promise in this Psalm to praise God forever for what He had done. God has done GREAT things for you too, praise Him.

Take time to praise God today. Praise Him by singing a song. Write the name of the song. Write down why God is special to you.

Nothing you can do would be good enough for you to earn your way to Heaven. You need a Savior. God has provided one. His name is Jesus.

Decode this message.

Go tell it on the mountain!

I will praise you forever for what you have done. In your name I will hope for your name is good. I will praise you in the presence of your saints

Everyone has turned away they have together become corrupt

There is no o who does good, not even one.

J E S U S
4 2 7 8 7

is the

S a v i o r
7 1 9 3 5 6

A=1; E=2; I=3; J=4; O=5; R=6; S=7; U=8; V=9

Pray
Continue to praise God today while you pray. Tell Him thanks.

Pray
Thank Jesus for dying for your sin.

WEDNESDAY Psalm 54:4

God will help you in all troubles, whether big or small. He wants to help you deal with the school bully. He wants to help you when you're afraid of the dark.

When you have troubles, one thing you can do is read God's Word and find the strength and wisdom you need. Match the sentences to the trouble they could help. Tomorrow's quiet time will give you another thing you can do when you have troubles!

Surely God is my help in the Lord is the one who sustains me.

love your enemies.

Pray Pray the Bible verse you read.

THURSDAY Psalm 55:1

When you need God's help, another thing you can do is go to Him in prayer and tell Him about your problems. He will hear and answer you.

Find and circle the hidden praying hands in this picture.

Listen to my prayer O God do not ignore my plea.

P. Sattler 4/17

Pray Tell God about your problem and ask Him to help you.

FRIDAY Psalm 55:22

The Bible is God's word to you. God promises to care for you. Remember to bring your troubles to God in prayer and read His Word. He promises He will take care of you.

God cares for you in so many different ways. He makes sure you have food to eat, clothes to wear, and a place to sleep. Match the word with the picture.

Sleep

Eat

Wear

God cares for

hear me and answer me. My thoughts trouble me and I am distraught

Pray Thank God for caring for you.

SATURDAY Psalm 56:3

Whenever you are afraid be like King David, trust in God, the King of kings.

Connect the dots and color the picture.

60
40
20
50   70
30
10

O
GOD

When I am afraid I will trust in you.

P. Sattler 4/17

Pray Ask God to help you trust Him in all things.

COMMENT CORNER
Parent or Leader, circle a comment and/or write your own.

You're special   You can do it   God loves you!   Nice job!   We're proud of you!   Keep it up

WOW!

DAYS COMPLETED
7

19

WEEK 2

SUNDAY
Psalm 57:5

When is God worthy to be praised? Start at the arrow and write every other letter of the blank.

_ _ _ _

_ _ _ _ _

_ _ _ _ _ _

"Glorious God"

How do you describe God? Who is He?

He is merciful and forgiving.

He is powerful and a fair judge.

He is caring and trustworthy.

Pray
Ask God to help you remember to praise Him even on bad days.

David praised God even in times of trouble. Remember God is good all the time. He is always worthy of our praise.

TUESDAY
Psalm 59:16

David loved to praise God and he often did it in song. In this verse, David praises God for being powerful, merciful, and his refuge (protection from danger).

God is many wonderful things. List 3 more praises about God. Praise Him for being these things. Can you make up your own praise song?

God is:

_____, _____, _____

My Song of praise

_____

_____

_____

MONDAY
Psalm 58:11

Everyone will realize that God is a fair judge and those who followed Him will be rewarded.

Pray
Tell God thank you for all the wonderful things He is.

Complete the following problems to help you remember today's lesson.

+ = _____

+ = _____

Pray
Thank God for being a fair judge. Pray that you will live as God wants.

WEDNESDAY — Psalm 60:11

Have you ever met a bully? Is there someone you can't seem to get along with? Would you call them your enemy? God is our only true help against our enemies.

Look up this Bible verse for God's help against your enemy. Matthew 5:44 What does God want you to do? Write your answer on the line.

God says to
l _ _ _ and p _ _ _
for our enemies.

Pray
Pray for the person who doesn't treat you kindly. Ask God to help you love them, as He loves them.

THURSDAY — Psalm 61:5

An inheritance is a gift someone gives you when they die. Jesus died on the cross for your sin. When you believe this, He gives you an inheritance of eternal life in Heaven.

Have you accepted Jesus as your Savior? Color in your answer.

NO   YES

Ask an adult from church or your parent to tell you how you can have Jesus as your Savior.

Say NO to sin and YES to Him!

Pray
Tell Jesus thank you for His gift to you.

FRIDAY — Psalm 62:1

Sin separates you from God and keeps you from Heaven. You need someone to take away your sin, to save you from punishment. Who is going to save you? God. Salvation (being saved from sin) comes only from God.

God came to earth as a man. His name was Jesus. He never sinned, yet He died on a cross as punishment for your sin. This is how God saves you when you believe Jesus did this for

Start

Heaven

Pray
Pray for the salvation of everyone.

SATURDAY — Psalm 63:6

Let God and who He is always be on your mind. Think about Him when you wake up, when you go to school, play, and when you go to bed.

Cross out what doesn't belong in each row.

   God

 God

 God

Pray
Ask God to always be on your mind.

COMMENT CORNER
Parent or Leader, circle a comment and/or write your own.

You're special   You can do it   God loves you!   Nice job!   We're proud of you!   Keep it up   WOW!

DAYS COMPLETED

21

WEEK 3

"Psalms of Pray"

The Bible can give you ideas to help you pray. You can even pray the verses back to God.

Last night, I read about how God protects me, so I prayed that God would keep me safe on my trip.

I read that we should thank God, so I take time every night to tell Him thank you.

I read that we should thank God, so I take time every night to tell Him thank you.

SUNDAY
Psalm 64:2

Find and circle these words in the word search.

GOD   PRAY   WICKED
HIDE   PROTECT

P	R	A	Y	B	C	N
P	R	N	G	O	R	S
P	E	O	P	G	E	T
J	D	H	T	C	B	R
W	I	C	K	E	D	A
E	H	G	Y	R	C	B
N	P	R	R	F	J	T

Like David, you can pray for God's protection from anything and everything.

Pray
Ask God to help you not be afraid.

TUESDAY
Psalm 66:16

Your days are filled with things God does for you. Take time to tell others about these wonderful things.

MONDAY
Psalm 65:3

Everyone has sinned and has an unclean heart. God will forgive all your sin; past, present, and future. How GREAT God is!

Unscramble this message.

dGo lliw giforve ouy.

G _ _   _ _ ll
_ _ r _ i _ e   y _ u.

Pray
Thank God that He forgives sin.

What has God done for you today? Has He answered a prayer? Did He bless you in a special way? Are you forgiven of your sin? Write a sentence or draw a picture of something God has done for you today. Tell someone about it.

Pray
Thank God for the things He has given you.

WEDNESDAY   Psalm 67:2

As a Christian, you should want the whole world to know of God and His gift of salvation.

Color this map of the world. Color the bodies of water **blue**. Color the continents **green**. Circle one of the continents in **red**. Can you name this continent? Pray for the people of this continent to learn about God.

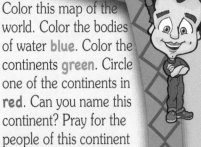

Pray

Pray for a missionary from your church.

THURSDAY   Psalm 68:2-3

King David says wicked people are like smoke or melting wax, things that don't last. The righteous, those who believe in Jesus, can rejoice and be happy.

Righteous and rejoice are words that describe eternity for those who believe in Jesus as their Savior. Righteous, rejoice, and reward all start with R. How many things can you find in this picture that start with R? Circle them.

Pray

Give thanks for Jesus, the Savior of the world.

FRIDAY   Psalm 68:19

Every day God cares for you and helps you with your problems. He has the answer to your biggest problem, sin. The solution is Jesus. This is just one reason why God is worthy of your worship.

Can you find the answer to this problem? Mrs. Roberts made 12 cupcakes. After school, John ate 2 cupcakes, Sara ate 2 cupcakes and Rachel ate 1 cupcake. How many cupcakes are left?

Pray

Ask God to help you with a problem you are having.

SATURDAY   Psalm 68:32

In Heaven, believers will sing praises to God. But you don't have to wait; you can sing praises to God every day.

Look at the two pictures of children singing praises to God. Circle the 5 differences you see in the pictures.

Pray

Thank God for your voice and that you can sing songs to Him.

COMMENT CORNER   Parent or Leader, circle a comment and/or write your own.

You're special   You can do it   God loves you!   Nice job!   We're proud of you!   Keep it up   WOW!

DAYS COMPLETED

23

WEEK 4

Can anyone tell me how to live for God?

Tell others about God.

Seek God by reading the Bible and praying.

Trust God when things are good or bad.

SUNDAY

Psalm 69:7

It is not fun when others are cruel to you. Be strong and continue to follow Jesus. He will reward you in Heaven for your faithfulness. Count by 2's to help this child climb over the rocks of cruelty to reach his reward.

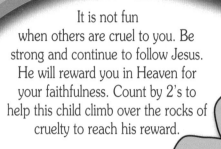

10

8   9

6   7

3   4   5

1   2

Just like King David, there might be times in your life when others will be cruel to you because you follow Jesus.

Pray
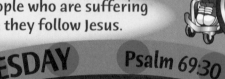
Pray for people who are suffering because they follow Jesus.

MONDAY

Psalm 69:13

TUESDAY

Psalm 69:30

When everyone was being cruel to David because he loved God, David didn't turn from God. Instead, David turned to God in prayer, knowing that God never stops loving him.

When you pray God doesn't have to say "yes", He can also say "no" or "wait". He loves and knows what is best for you. Trust Him. Can you match the symbols with their meanings?

When God does something great for you, you should take time to praise Him and give Him thanks. God is worthy of all of your praise and thanks.

Sing a song of praise to God today. Make a list of all the things for which you can thank God.

Thank You God.

Wait
Go/Yes
Stop/No

1. _____

2. _____

3. _____

Pray
Ask for something today, and then wait patiently for His answer. Write it or draw it in your prayer journal.

Pray

Tell God thank you.

WEDNESDAY — Psalm 70:4

Seek God. Study His Word, pray, and attend church. As you learn more about God, you will be glad and want to rejoice. "Great is the Lord!"

Find the 5 hidden Bibles in this picture.

Pray
Pray that you will always want to know more about God.

THURSDAY — Psalm 71:8

While it is important to take a special time every day, to read God's Word and pray. You shouldn't just think of God during this time. You should be praising Him all day in your thoughts, actions, and words.

Crack the code to uncover when you should praise God.

A=12:00; D=2:00; E=4:00; L=6:00;
R=8:00; V=10:00; Y=11:00

Pray
Thank God for giving you this day to praise Him in all you do.

FRIDAY — Psalm 71:15

When you tell others about God, you can tell them He is perfect. He never sins. He is righteous.

Tell your friends that Jesus took the punishment for everyone's sin. If we believe, we can live in Heaven with Him someday. How many friends has each child told about Jesus?

Pray
Thank God for your mind, your mouth, your ears, and your eyes.

SATURDAY — Psalm 72:1

It is good to pray for the leaders of your country, just as the author of this Psalm prayed for the king.

Color your country's flag as you remember to pray for the leaders today.

Pray
Pray for your country's leaders to be wise and make good decisions.

COMMENT CORNER
Parent or Leader, circle a comment and/or write your own.

You're special · You can do it · God loves you! · Nice job! · We're proud of you! · Keep it up · WOW!

DAYS COMPLETED

25

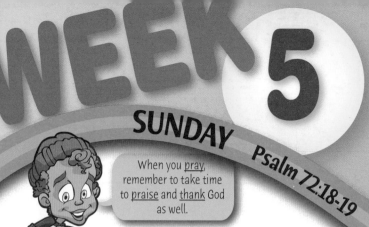

WEEK 5

"God is..."

God is praiseworthy.

God is always with me.

God is faithful.

God is wonderful beyond my imagination!

SUNDAY — Psalm 72:18-19

When you <u>pray</u>, remember to take time to <u>praise</u> and <u>thank</u> God as well.

Finish the puzzle.

Pray
Start your prayer praising God, ask Him for what you need, and end your prayer praising Him again.

MONDAY — Psalm 73:3

Sometimes you may see good things happening to people who are unsaved, while you are struggling. This might make you feel jealous and wonder why you are following God. Stay faithful to God remembering your rewards will be forever in Heaven. The things on earth will end.

Draw lines to show which things will be forever and which will end.

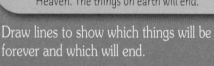

Heaven

Heavenly rewards

Forever End

Pray
Ask God to help you follow Him even when it's hard.

TUESDAY — Psalm 73:23-24

When you are a child of God, you are always with God and God is always with you. He never leaves. God is always with you to guide and to help you.

Can you show these children the way home? Remember God is always with you showing you the right way.

Pray
Thank God for being with you forever and always

WEDNESDAY Psalm 74:1

When you are behaving sinfully, it can feel as though God is angry with you. Remember God hates sin and it separates you from Him. If God feels far away, stop and pray, asking God to show you where you might be sinning. Confess your sin and God will forgive you.

What separates you from God? Find the answer by writing the first letter of each word.

____ ____ ____

Pray

Confess your sin. Tell God you're sorry.

FRIDAY Psalm 75:7

God is the Judge. He decides right from wrong. You learn what is right or wrong by reading God's Word.

Draw a line to the opposites.

Wrong   High

Low   Bottom

Up   Down

Top   Right

Pray

Ask God to help you learn from the Bible what is right and wrong.

THURSDAY Psalm 74:16-17

God made the day and the night, the sun and the moon. He created summer and winter. He is God and He will be a King forever.

Complete the bar graph.

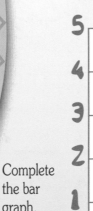

Pray

Thank God for creating your favorite season.

SATURDAY Psalm 76:4

Who is most wonderful and magnificent? Hold this page up to a mirror to find the answer. Write it on the line.

____ ____ ____

Pray

Tell God how wonderful He is.

COMMENT CORNER Parent or Leader, circle a comment and/or write your own.

You're special   You can do it   God loves you!   Nice job!   We're proud of you!   Keep it up   WOW!

DAYS COMPLETED

27

"A Servant's Heart"

What can we do to serve God?

Obey His Word.

Thank Him for what He provides.

Be a helper at church.

SUNDAY
1 Timothy 1:8

Decode the message to complete the sentence.

God's law is found in the

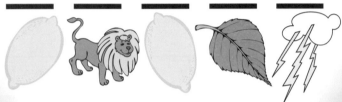

B = (lemon) E = (lightning) I = (lion) L = (leaf)

God's law is good. It is good to obey His law.

Pray
Thank God for your Bible. Ask Him to help you obey His Word.

MONDAY
1 Timothy 1:15

Jesus came to earth to save sinners. You are a sinner because you do, say, or think things that disobey God. Jesus came to save you.

Circle the word Yes or No for each statement.

1. You are a sinner. **YES NO**

2. Jesus came to save you. **YES NO**

3. You have asked Jesus to save you from your sin. **YES NO**

If no, talk to your parents or an adult at church.

Pray
Ask Jesus to help you not sin.

TUESDAY
1 Timothy 2:3-4

God wants everyone to be saved. He wants you to know the truth about His Son, Jesus.

Solve the code to see who God wants to be saved.

E = (child)   R = (man)
N = (child with toy)   V = (girl)
O = (man in suit)   Y = (child with bag)

Pray
Ask God to help you tell others how they can be saved from their sin.

28

WEDNESDAY 1 Timothy 2:8

God does not want you to argue with others. Instead, you should get along with one another and pray together.

When you are arguing with someone, you cannot pray to God. Color the picture of what God wants you to do.

Pray

Take time today to pray with a friend or family member.

THURSDAY 1 Timothy 3:1

God says that it is a very good choice for a man to become a pastor.

Circle the pastor. Find 4 hidden Bibles and circle them. Write your pastor's name on the line.

_____
Pastor's name

Pray

Ask God to help your pastor today.

FRIDAY 1 Timothy 3:13

Deacons help at church by serving and caring for others. God blesses them for their work. You can be a helper at home and at church.

Draw a line to connect the word on the left with the words on the right that match to show how you can be a helper.

Helping

pick up toys

throw trash on floor

pray for others

Not Helping

argue

say "thank you"

Pray Thank God for the deacons or helpers at your church.

SATURDAY 1 Timothy 4:4

God wants you to be thankful for everything He gives to you. You can be thankful for your food.

Hold this page in front of a mirror and write the word in the blank.

To thank God for your food you should _____ before you eat.

YAЯP

Pray Today at mealtime tell Jesus thank you for your food.

COMMENT CORNER
Parent or Leader, circle a comment and/or write your own.

You're special   You can do it   God loves you!   Nice job!   We're proud of you!   Keep it up   WOW!

DAYS COMPLETED

29

WEEK 7

"Helping Hands"

Wow, God has a lot to say about how we should use our money!

We should share with others.

We can also take care of older people because they need our help.

Find and circle the five words in the puzzle.

```
A F B C N A Y W
V O A T Q L V O
A C T I O N S R
P U R I T Y N D
L O V E P H V S
```

ACTIONS FAITH LOVE
PURITY WORDS

1 Timothy 4:12

Even though you are young, you can still be an example to others with your words (what you say), actions (what you do), love (kind to all), faith (trust in God), and purity (right before God).

Pray
Ask God to help you be an example to others.

MONDAY

1 Timothy 5:3

A widow is a woman whose husband has died. God wants the people in the church to help and care for the widows.

Circle the pictures that show the things you can do to help a widow.

TUESDAY

1 Timothy 5:9

Paul told Timothy to make a list of the widows that were more than sixty years old. These were the women the church should help.

Make a list of two widows in your church or neighborhood that you can help. Write one thing you can do to help these widows.

1. _____
2. _____
3. _____

Pray Ask God to help you find ways to help a widow in your church or neighborhood.

Pray
Thank God for the people in your church who help take care of widows.

WEDNESDAY — 1 Timothy 5:17

You should honor the preachers and teachers in your church by obeying, thanking, and helping them.

Color the pieces with the dots to see how you should treat your pastor.

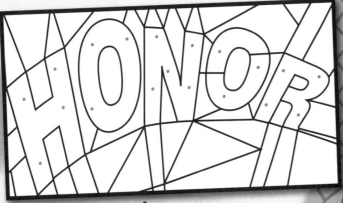

Pray: Ask God to help your pastor and teachers as they get ready to teach you on Sunday.

THURSDAY — 1 Timothy 6:7

You should not try to get lots of things on earth because you cannot take them with you when you die. Instead, you can spend your time and money on things that please God.

Draw lines from the clock and money to whom you should please with your time and money.

God   Me

Pray: Ask God to help you use your time and money to please Him.

FRIDAY — 1 Timothy 6:10

The Bible says loving money will cause bad things to happen. You can please God by loving Him instead of money.

Under each picture circle the word that pleases God.

GOD

GOOD BAD

GOOD BAD

Pray: Tell God how much you love him. Ask Him to help you love Him more and love money less.

SATURDAY — 1 Timothy 6:18

God wants you to do good things for Him. He wants you to share what you have with others who are in need.

Write the word in the blank to finish the rhyme.

I show that I care

when I _ _ _ _ _

A = 🍎   E = ✏️   H = 🧸

R = 🍬   S = 🏀

Pray: Ask God to show you something you have that you can share with someone.

COMMENT CORNER — Parent or Leader, circle a comment and/or write your own.

You're special   You can do it   God loves you!   Nice job!   We're proud of you!   Keep it up   WOW!

DAYS COMPLETED

31

WEEK 8

"Best is Best"

How can we give God our best?

Giving Him our heart.

Obeying His Word.

Showing love to others.

SUNDAY — Leviticus 1:2

The best way to give God your heart is by obeying and following His Word. Color the heart that belongs to God.

obey
love
patience
joy

disobey
selfish
hate
anger

The Israelites were to give God an offering. God expects offerings from His children. The best offering you can give God is your heart.

Pray
Tell God you would like to give Him your heart.

MONDAY — Leviticus 5:6

Sins of the Israelites needed a special sin offering. God gave you the best sin offering by sending His Son, Jesus.

Unscramble the letters and place them on the cross to reveal God's offering to you.

Pray
Thank God for the offering of His Son, Jesus.

TUESDAY — Leviticus 17:11

Before Jesus came to earth, animals were sacrificed. Jesus shed His blood for your sin. Animals aren't needed anymore.

Color the triangles red to take the children to who shed His blood for their sin.

Start

Jesus

Pray
Thank Jesus for dying on the cross for you.

32

WEDNESDAY
Leviticus 19:18

When God talks about your neighbor, He means everyone. You are to treat everyone the way you would want to be treated.

Circle the things that are showing love.

Take the biggest cookie for yourself.

Wait your turn.

Share your snack.

Shove to the front of the line.

Help your friend clean up a mess.

Keep the best toys for yourself.

Drop your trash on the floor.

Pray
Ask God to help you show love to others today.

THURSDAY
Leviticus 20:26

God has made those who believe in Him to be holy. That makes you special to God.

God made you special so you can be useful to Him. These words are things you can do to be useful to God. Find them in the word search.

OBEY PRAY SHARE

E	Y	T	Z	P
K	R	E	R	Y
N	V	A	B	O
M	Y	X	H	O
O	U	U	K	S

Pray
Thank God for taking care of you.

FRIDAY
Leviticus 22:18-19

God gave His best, Jesus. God wants only your best not your second best.

Insert the vowels to read the message.

G_v_ G_d

Y__r B_st.

e =  elephant   i = igloo   o = ostrich   u = umbrella

Pray
Ask God to help you give Him your best.

SATURDAY
Leviticus 23:4

God's people had special days to celebrate and remember what God did for them.

Easter

Thanksgiving

Birthday

Christmas

Draw a line from the picture to the holiday that you can celebrate to remember what God did for you.

Pray
Thank God for special holidays to remember Him.

COMMENT CORNER
Parent or Leader, circle a comment and/or write your own.

You're special   You can do it   God loves you!   Nice job!   We're proud of you!   Keep it up   WOW!

DAYS COMPLETED

33

WEEK 9

SUNDAY — Leviticus 23:18

"Don't Worry, be Happy!"

God likes us to be happy.

I'm happy He made me.

I'm happy I have a home in Heaven.

I'm happy He sent Jesus.

14 16
12 18 20
10
8
6 24 22
4 2

The Lamb of God, Jesus, died for your sin. Count by two's and draw a line from 2 to 24. Color the lamb.

The Israelites had to sacrifice a perfect lamb. Jesus is the Lamb of God who died for your sin.

Pray

Thank God for sending Jesus to die for your sin.

MONDAY — Leviticus 23:24

The Israelites celebrated the Feast of the Trumpets. Some day a trumpet will sound and those who believe in Jesus will go to Heaven!

Check your answers in the boxes. If you wrote no, talk to your parent or an adult at church about how you can go to Heaven.

Do you believe Jesus died for your sin? ☐ YES ☐ NO

Will you go to Heaven to live with Jesus forever? ☐ YES ☐ NO

Pray

Thank God for Heaven.

TUESDAY — Leviticus 23:40

The Bible is God's word to you. God promises to care for you. Remember to bring your troubles to God in prayer and read His Word. He promises He will take care of you.

Will you choose to rejoice or be grumpy today? Fill in the blanks to spell out the best choice.

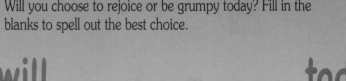

I will _ _ _ _ _ _ _ toda

e j r e i o c

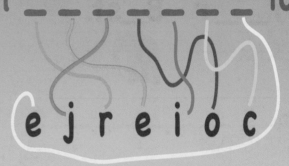

no matter what happens.

Pray Sing a song to God thanking Him for loving you.

WEDNESDAY — Leviticus 25:10

Jubilee celebrated freedom. Freedom was given to those who were slaves. Jubilee reminded the people of living in Heaven.

Follow the path that takes the people to Heaven.

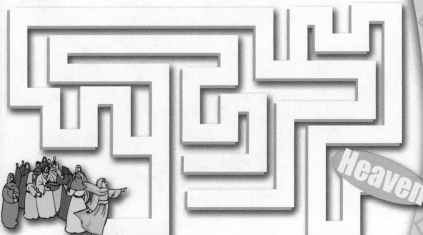

Heaven

Pray
Thank God that He made a way for you to go to Heaven someday.

THURSDAY — Leviticus 26:12

God wants to be your God. He loves you so much!

How much do you love God? Color the heart that shows how much you love Him. Write or draw one thing you do to show Him you love Him.

_____

Pray
Thank God for His great love for you.

FRIDAY — Leviticus 26:18

When you do not obey God's rules, it is called sin. God has to punish those who do not obey Him. The punishment for sin is to be separated from God.

You need to obey God. Match the word on the left to the result on the right.

SIN   BLESSING

OBEDIENCE   PUNISHMENT

Pray
Ask God to help you listen and obey His Word.

SATURDAY — Leviticus 26:45

God always keeps His Word. He will never break a promise.

What about you? Do you always do what you say you will do? Use the three words to fill in the shapes.

Word

trust

truth

You must tell the ▲ .

You can ● God.

God's ▬ is true.

Pray
Thank God for keeping His promises.

COMMENT CORNER
Parent or Leader, circle a comment and/or write your own.

You're special   You can do it   God loves you!   Nice job!   We're proud of you!   Keep it up   WOW!

DAYS COMPLETED

35

WEEK 10

Jesus came to earth not just to do miracles.

He came to take away our sins.

And give us power to not sin.

SUNDAY
Mark 1:13

Satan wanted Jesus to sin. He wants you to sin, too. Jesus has power to help you say no. All you have to do is ask Him.

Fill in the prayer to God asking Him for <u>help</u> to do what is <u>right</u>.

Dear God, Please h _ _ _ me to do the r _ gh _ things today and not the wrong things. In Jesus' name, Amen.

Pray
Ask Jesus to help you say no to sin and yes to Him.

MONDAY
Mark 1:17

Peter, Andrew, James, and John left everything to follow Jesus. He wants you to follow, too. Obeying is one way to follow Jesus.

Color the picture to remind you to follow Jesus.

Pray
Ask Jesus to help you be His follower.

TUESDAY
Mark 1:35

Prayer was important to Jesus. It should be important to you, too.

Mark off each day that you will pray this week.

Name _____

- ☐ Sunday
- ☐ Monday
- ☐ Tuesday
- ☐ Wednesday
- ☐ Thursday
- ☐ Friday
- ☐ Saturday

Pray
Ask God to help you to remember to pray.

WEDNESDAY — Mark 1:45

Jesus healed the leper. He was so happy he told everyone what Jesus had done. Do you tell others about Jesus?

Who can you tell about Jesus? Write every other letter on the blanks to find out. Start with the letter E.

E A V B E W R T Y O B P O H D N Y

_ _ _ _ _ _ _ _ _ _ _ _

Pray

Ask God who you can tell about Jesus.

THURSDAY — Mark 2:10

Jesus said He has power to forgive sins.

Check the box yes or no to answer the questions.

	YES	NO
Do you believe that Jesus died for your sins?	☐	☐
Do you believe that Jesus rose from the dead?	☐	☐
Do you believe that Jesus will be alive forever?	☐	☐
Do you know Jesus as your Savior?	☐	☐

Pray

Thank Jesus that He can forgive your sins.

FRIDAY — Mark 2:14-15

Matthew left everything and followed Jesus. Matthew was Jesus' friend.

Follow the prints to help Matthew follow Jesus.

Pray

Tell Jesus thank you for being your friend.

SATURDAY — Mark 3:5

Jesus is sad when people have hard hearts. A hard heart doesn't believe in Jesus.

Color the soft heart red, color the hard heart black. Circle the kind of heart that you have.

I believe in Jesus.

I don't believe.

Pray

Ask Jesus to help you have a right heart with Him.

COMMENT CORNER

Parent or Leader, circle a comment and/or write your own.

You're special   You can do it   God loves you!   Nice Job!   We're proud of you!   Keep it up   WOW!

DAYS COMPLETED

37

WEEK 11

"Follow Him"

Jesus had 12 special friends.

They were called disciples.

I want to be a disciple of Jesus!

SUNDAY
Mark 3:14

Find the group that shows halves. Write ½ under each part.

_____

_____

Jesus chose 12 special men to be His disciples. A disciple is someone who learns.

Pray
Thank Jesus for being your friend.

MONDAY
Mark 3:35

When you do God's will and believe in Him, you are in His family.

Follow the path to find out how to be in God's family.

Your name

Jesus

Family of God

Pray
Thank God for being in His family.

TUESDAY
Mark 4:9

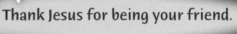

Jesus wants you to use your ears to hear His truths.

Find the 4 hidden ears and 5 hidden Bibles.

Pray
Thank God for your ears.

WEDNESDAY — Mark 4:21

You are to be a light for Jesus and shine His love so others may see.

Find 5 things that give light and circle them. Draw a square around the one that will show you how to shine.

Pray
Ask God to help you shine today.

THURSDAY — Mark 4:41

The big storm was stopped when Jesus said to be still. If the wind and sea obey Him, so should you.

Connect the dots. Start with 5 and count by 5's.

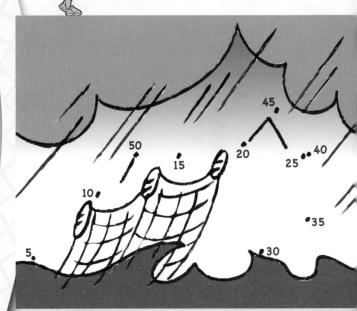

Pray
Ask God to help you obey today.

FRIDAY — Mark 5:6

Even though Jesus was far away, the man worshipped Him. Jesus is in Heaven, but He's always close for you to worship and praise Him.

Color the last musical note in each line to finish the pattern.

Pray Praise God for all He has done for you.

SATURDAY — Mark 5:19

You are to tell others about the great things Jesus has done for you.

Check the ways you can share Jesus with others.

____ **Share your testimony.**

____ Ignore people.

____ **Be a good friend.**

____ Ask someone to church.

____ Fight with others.

Pray Ask Jesus to help you tell others about Him.

COMMENT CORNER
Parent or Leader, circle a comment and/or write your own.

You're special You can do it God loves you! Nice job! We're proud of you! Keep it up WOW!

DAYS COMPLETED

"Believe It"

Jesus did many miracles.

I believe it.

Believing is called faith.

It was proof that He was God.

SUNDAY
Mark 5:27-28

Follow each line to find the letters you need to put in each numbered circle.

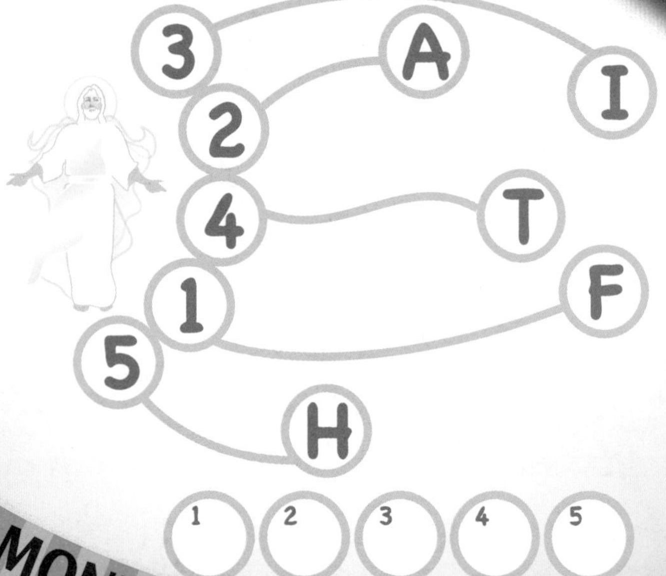

3
2
4
1
5

A
I
T
F
H

1 2 3 4 5

This woman was sick for years. She knew if she just touched Jesus' clothes, she would be healed. That was great faith.

Pray
Ask God to help you have faith.

MONDAY
Mark 5:42

The little girl was dead, but Jesus brought her back to life.

What does Jesus have? Color the triangles. Then copy those letters in the triangle below to find out.

P
E
W
R
O

TUESDAY
Mark 6:12

Jesus sent His twelve disciples out to tell others about Him. Jesus wants you to tell others, too.

Count by twos from 2 to 12. Color these numbers to show the path the disciples took to tell others about Jesus.

2	4	9	22
11	6	8	18
17	20	10	12

Pray
Thank Jesus for His power.

Pray
Ask Jesus to help you tell others about Him.

40

WEDNESDAY   Mark 6:15

Some people were confused about who Jesus was. You can know Jesus is God's Son because you have the Bible.

God's truth is found in the Bible. Color the Bibles that contain lower case letters. Then copy the CAPITAL letters to the spaces below.

Pray
Tell God thank you for His Word, the Bible.

__ __ __ __ __

THURSDAY   Mark 6:41

Jesus thanked God for the food. You should pray and thank God each time you eat for the food He gives you.

Read the clues. Mark the chart with ✻'s. Write a person's name under each meal.

1. Everyone had fruit
2. Mr. Marc and Alex had toast.
3. Joey had cereal.
4. Joey and Alex had juice.
5. Mr. Marc had milk.

	milk	juice	fruit	cereal	toast
Mr. Marc					
Alex					
Joey					

Pray   Thank God for your food.

FRIDAY   Mark 6:50

Jesus told the disciples not to be afraid. He is always ready to help. If you are afraid, ask God to help you.

Write or draw one thing that frightens you. Ask God to protect you from your fear.

Pray
Ask God to help you when you are frightened.

SATURDAY   Mark 7:8

The Pharisees cared more about their rules than God. God wants you to love Him more than anything else.

Underline what you are to love the most.

Friends
TV
Toys
God
Pets

Pray
Ask God to help you love Him more than anything.

COMMENT CORNER
Parent or Leader, circle a comment and/or write your own.

You're special   You can do it   God loves you!   Nice job!   We're proud of you!   Keep it up   WOW!

DAYS COMPLETED

WEEK 13

"Who is this Man?"

Some people thought he was Elijah.

I know who He is! He's God's Son, the Savior!

Many people didn't know who Jesus was.

Some thought he was a good teacher.

SUNDAY
Mark 7:14

Follow the path to help Joey find understanding.

God wants you to hear so you can understand. Understanding helps you to obey. You will find understanding in God's Word.

Pray
Ask God to help you to hear so you can have understanding.

MONDAY
Mark 7:37

Jesus healed the deaf man. Now he could hear God's Word!

Circle the ways you can hear God's Word.

pastor

TV

computer

parents

Sunday school teacher

Pray
Tell God thank you for ears that hear.

TUESDAY
Mark 8:2

Jesus had compassion on the hungry people. Compassion means you care. You need to care about others' needs.

Draw food on the plate you can share with others.

Pray
Ask God to help you share with others.

WEDNESDAY — Mark 8:11

The Pharisees did not want to believe that Jesus is the Savior. Not everybody believes. You can pray for those people.

Write the letter that comes after each letter to find the hidden message.

I D R T R   H R

_ _ _ _ _   _ _

S G D   R Z U H N Q.

_ _ _   _ _ _ _ _ _ _.

Pray

Pray for those people who don't believe in Jesus.

THURSDAY — Mark 8:29

Not everybody knows who Jesus is. Peter knew that He was the Christ, the Savior. Do you know who Jesus is?

Hold this page in front of a mirror to see the message. Fill in the answer from the message.

Savior

Jesus is the

_ _ _ _ _ _.

Pray

Thank God for sending Jesus to be the Savior.

FRIDAY — Mark 9:7

God said Jesus is His Son and everyone needs to listen to Him.

Answer the questions and fill in the crossword puzzle.

Everyone
Bible
Savior

Across
3. Who is Jesus?

Down
1. Who needs to listen to Jesus?
2. Where can I learn about Jesus?

Pray

Thank God for sending His Son Jesus.

SATURDAY — Mark 9:24

This father asked Jesus to help him believe. You can always ask Jesus for help. He is ready to give it.

Color the picture that shows what to do when you need God's help.

Pray

Thank God for all His help.

COMMENT CORNER

Parent or Leader, circle a comment and write your own.

You're special   You can do it   God loves you!   Nice job!   We're proud of you!   Keep it up   WOW!

43

WEEK 14

"Servant of All"

Did you know that Jesus came to serve?

Jesus put others first.

I want to be a servant like Jesus.

He was our example.

Fill in the circles to find out what you should do.

I n__d t_b_ J_s_s' h_lp_r.

e o u

SUNDAY — Mark 9:34

The disciples argued about who would be the most important. Jesus said that whoever was His Helper was what was important. To be Jesus' helper is the greatest thing!

Pray
Ask God to help you be a helper.

MONDAY — Mark 9:50

God wants you to be at peace with each other. You can be a peacemaker by not arguing with others.

Under each picture write an action word from the box.

climb
dig
slide
jump

Pray
Ask God to help you be a peacemaker.

TUESDAY — Mark 10:14

Jesus loves children and wants them to come to Him. Jesus loves you and wants you to come to Him!

Are you Jesus' child? Have you asked Him to be your Savior from sin? Color the heart that answers the question. If no, talk to your parent or an adult at church.

yes

no

Pray
Tell Jesus thank you for wanting you to come to Him.

WEDNESDAY — Mark 10:24-25

You can't trust in money to get you to Heaven. There's only one way to Heaven and that is believing in Jesus.

Heaven

How many ways are there to Heaven? Complete the maze to find out.

Pray

Tell God you are thankful for Heaven.

THURSDAY — Mark 10:45

Jesus came to earth to be a servant. He served you by dying for your sin.

Follow the lines to fill in the blanks.

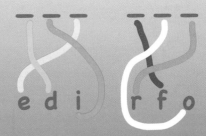

To _ _ _ _ _ _
    e d i   r f o

my _ _ _.
      n s i

Pray

Thank Jesus for being a servant and dying for you.

FRIDAY — Mark 10:52

Jesus healed the blind man. He was so happy that he followed Jesus and loved Him.

Color the squares with eyes to help the man follow Jesus.

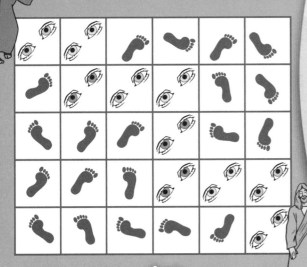

Pray

Tell God thank you for your eyes.

SATURDAY — Mark 11:9

The people praised Jesus as He rode into Jerusalem on a donkey. Jesus deserves your praise.

Find the hidden palm branches in the picture and circle them.

Pray

Praise God for something He has done.

COMMENT CORNER

Parent or Leader, circle a comment and/or write your own.

You're special   You can do it   God loves you!   Nice job!   We're proud of you!   Keep it up   WOW!

DAYS COMPLETED

45

WEEK 15

The Greatest Commandment

God said we are to love Him.

With all our heart.

And with all our soul.

With all our strength.

With all our mind.

SUNDAY

Mark 11:17

God's house (church) is to be place of prayer and worship, not a place for lying, stealing, and other bad things.

Color the picture of the church using the color code.

red
green
yellow
blue

Pray
Thank God for your church.

MONDAY

Mark 11:25

It is important to forgive others so God can forgive you.

Circle the red letters and write them on the blanks to find out what to do.

S J T F B H O D R
Z G I U I Y H V F
E J O L T E R H O
E S A R P Q S

_ _ _ _ _ _ _ _ _
_ _ _ _ _ _

Pray
Ask God to help you forgive others.

TUESDAY

Mark 12:12

The Pharisees wanted to destroy Jesus because He spoke the truth.

Don't be like the Pharisees. Listen when people correct you. Find the 6 wrong things in the picture.

Pray
Ask God to help you listen and obey.

46

WEDNESDAY — Mark 12:17

The people were told to pay their taxes to the king and to give their tithes to God. Tithes are gifts you give to God.

Check off things you can give to Jesus.

- ☐ **Your time**
- ☐ **Your money**
- ☐ **Your helping hands**
- ☐ **Your heart**

Pray
Ask God to help you give an offering this week.

THURSDAY — Mark 12:29-31

Jesus said the two most important things to do are to love God with all your heart and to love your neighbor.

Number the pictures to show what order they should be in your life.

Pray
Ask God who you can show love to today.

FRIDAY — Mark 13:5

Jesus warns that some people will tell lies about Him. You need to learn God's Word so you won't be tricked.

Circle two things you can do to know more about Jesus.

Memorize Bible verses.

Read the Bible.

Watch TV.

Play with friends.

Pray
Ask God to help you learn more about Him.

SATURDAY — Mark 13:21

Some people will say that Jesus is here on earth. Don't believe them! Jesus is in Heaven.

Fill in the blanks with the first letter of each picture to find out where Jesus lives.

_____

Pray
Ask Jesus to help you know the truth.

COMMENT CORNER
Parent or Leader, circle a comment and/or write your own.

You're special · You can do it · God loves you! · Nice job! · We're proud of you! · Keep it up · WOW!

DAYS COMPLETED

47

WEEK 16

"Behold the Lamb"

He took the punishment for us.

Jesus is called the Lamb of God.

He came to die for our sin.

I love Him so much!

SUNDAY — Mark 13:33

Circle the ways you can be ready for Jesus.

You have to be ready when Jesus comes again! Live each day like it is the day He's coming.

Pray
Ask Jesus to help you be ready when He comes.

MONDAY — Mark 14:6

Jesus said Mary did a good work for Him. You can do good works for Jesus, too.

What can you do for Jesus? Copy the letters along the path into the boxes to find the answer.

G O K W S D O R O

Pray
Ask God to help you do good works today.

TUESDAY

The disciples were busy getting ready for the Passover. Jesus is the Passover Lamb.

Count by 2's to complete the dot to dot.

14• •16
10 12• •18 2
8 6
4• •2

Pray
Thank Jesus for being the Passover Lamb.

48

WEDNESDAY — Mark 14:23

Jesus shed His blood for your sins. It is important to never forget what Jesus did.

Have you asked Jesus to be your Savior from your sin? Circle your answer and follow the path to find out what you should do next.

YES — **NO**

Tell someone about your belief in Jesus.

Talk to your parents or a church leader to find out more about Jesus.

Pray
Tell God thank you for Jesus dying on the cross for you.

THURSDAY — Mark 14:35

Jesus had a hard thing to do. He prayed for power to help Him. God will give you strength to do hard things.

GOD HEARS PRAY STRENGTH

Find and circle the words in the puzzle.

S P V I
T R A H V
R A Y E M
E Y V A P
N U R H
G U S D
T O E R
H L D Q

Pray
Thank God for hearing your prayers.

FRIDAY — Mark 14:48

Jesus is all powerful and could have stopped the men, but He needed to suffer for your sin.

Start at the arrow. Write every other letter on blanks.

Z J E J B P I O H W E E K R S F N U G L Y M U E Z

Jesus is all

_ _ _ _ _ _ _ _ _'

Pray
Tell Jesus thank you for His great love for you.

SATURDAY — Mark 14:65

Jesus let Himself be spit upon and beaten because He was taking your punishment.

Trace the cross and write your name on it to remember what Jesus did for you.

Pray
Thank God for taking the punishment you deserved.

COMMENT CORNER
Parent or Leader, circle a comment and/or write your own.

You're special   You can do it   God loves you!   Nice job!   We're proud of you!   Keep it up   WOW!

DAYS COMPLETED

49

WEEK 17

"Amazing Love"

SUNDAY

Mark 14:72

Are you sorry when you do wrong? Finish the face to show how you should feel.

I am so glad that Jesus loves me so much to die on the cross.

His love for us is amazing!

I am so glad He is alive and in Heaven.

Peter denied Jesus 3 times. He said he didn't know Him. Peter was very sorry.

Pray

Ask God to help you say you're sorry when you need to.

MONDAY

Mark 15:14

TUESDAY

Mark 15:25

Pilate could find no wrong in Jesus, but the people wanted Jesus to die. Jesus did nothing wrong. He loved you so much He wanted to pay the price for your sin.

Draw a line to the correct answers.

Did Jesus do wrong?

Why did Jesus die?

Who can forgive sins?

Jesus

No

For my sins.

Jesus died on the cross for your sin. He took your punishment because He loves you.

Color the sun and clouds black to see what it looked like on the day Jesus died.

Pray

Thank Jesus for dying for your sin.

Pray

Thank Jesus for His wonderful love.

50

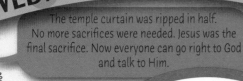

WEDNESDAY — Mark 15:38

The temple curtain was ripped in half. No more sacrifices were needed. Jesus was the final sacrifice. Now everyone can go right to God and talk to Him.

You can go straight to God. There is nothing in the way. Complete the maze to get to God.

Pray Thank God that you can pray to Him and have your sin forgiven.

THURSDAY — Mark 15:43

Joseph loved Jesus so much, he was not afraid to ask Pilate for Jesus' body after He died. Joseph even used his own tomb for Jesus.

Circle the name of the person who owned the tomb. Put a square around the name of who would be put in the tomb.

Joseph   Jesus

Pray Ask God to help you when you are afraid.

FRIDAY — Mark 16:6

The tomb was empty! Jesus is alive! What good news. The angel told the women to go and tell. Who can you tell the Good News to?

Color the picture. Write the name of someone you can tell on the empty tomb.

Pray Thank God for raising Jesus from the dead!

SATURDAY — Mark 16:19-20

After Jesus went to Heaven, the disciples went and preached everywhere. If you know Jesus as your Savior, you should tell others about Him, too.

Put a check next to the places where you can tell others about Jesus.

☐ My school
☐ The store
☐ The playground
☐ The library

Pray Ask Jesus to help you tell others about Him.

COMMENT CORNER

Parent or Leader, circle a comment and/or write your own.

You're special   You can do it   God loves you!   Nice job!   We're proud of you!   Keep it up   WOW!

DAYS COMPLETED

51

"Light and Dark"

Light means someone is doing the right things and obeying God.

Dark means someone is doing wrong things and disobeying God.

In the Bible when the words light and dark are used, what is the meaning?

SUNDAY 1 John 1:4

Write the name or draw a picture of someone you can encourage or bring joy to today. When you have talked to that person, color the star yellow.

I can encourage.

John wrote this letter to encourage and bring joy to the readers.

Pray
Ask God to help you bring joy to others.

MONDAY 1 John 1:5-7

John writes to the Christians to walk in the light. He wanted them to obey God. If you know Jesus as your Savior, you need to be careful to obey Him.

If you know Jesus, draw a picture of yourself on the white side of the page. If you do not know Jesus, draw yourself on the dark side of the page and talk to your parent or a leader at church about how you can know Jesus.

I know Jesus as my Savior.

I do not know Jesus as my Savior.

Pray
Thank Jesus that you can know Him and walk in the light.

TUESDAY 1 John 2:3

By obeying Jesus you are showing your love for Him. How can you tell if you really love Jesus?

Find out how by going around the path twice. Put every letter in a circle on the line. Then go back and use every letter in a square.

START ▶ I S S U H S O B W

E
M
J
I
R
H
O G F N E I V Y O E

Y
M
C
Y
E
L

_ ____ __ _____

___ _____

__ _____ ____.

Pray
Ask Jesus to help you obey Him today.

WEDNESDAY 1 John 2:10

When you love others, you are in the light (being obedient to Jesus). When you hate others, it is like being in the dark (sin).

You should act with love toward others. Check off the right ways to act toward others.

Pray

Ask Jesus to help you love others.

FRIDAY 1 John 2:21

Reading your Bible will help you know what is true. Everything written in the Bible is true. God's Word is true.

Count by 5's starting with the number 5 to find where you can know what is true.

15
50
20
40   45
25
BIBLE
55
60   10
35   5
30

Pray

Tell God thank you that His Word is true.

THURSDAY 1 John 2:17

Things on the earth will not last forever, but if you know Jesus, you have the hope of living with Him in Heaven forever.

Cross out the pictures of the things that will pass away. If you know that you will live in Heaven forever someday, draw line underneath the boy or girl.

Pray

Ask Jesus to help you know if you will live in Heaven someday.

SATURDAY 1 John 2:25

If you have believed in Jesus, that He died on the cross for your sin and rose again, Jesus promises you will be in Heaven with Him forever.

There is only one way to Heaven. You must believe Jesus died on the cross for your sin and rose again. If you believe that Jesus did this for you, draw a line from the children to the word Heaven.

HEAVEN

Pray

Tell Jesus thank you for dying for your sin.

COMMENT CORNER
Parent or Leader, circle a comment and/or write your own.

You're special   You can do it   God loves you!   Nice job!   We're proud of you!   Keep it up   WOW!

DAYS COMPLETED

53

WEEK 19

There is so much to learn about love this week!

God loves us so much.

He even calls us sons and daughters.

We can show God's love to others.

SUNDAY
1 John 2:28

Are you pleasing Jesus all day? Write 1, 2, and 3 next to the picture in the order you do them each day.

Jesus may return at any time. You should live to please Him everyday.

Pray

Ask Jesus to help you please Him every day.

TUESDAY
1 John 3:11

Jesus wants you to love other people, no matter what.

Write a name in each heart of someone you should love. Then color the hearts **red** or **pink**

MONDAY
1 John 3:4-5

Jesus lived on the earth in a body like yours, but He never sinned. That's because He is God's Son. God sent Jesus to earth to take away your sin.

Use the vowel code to complete the sentence.

G_d   s_nt   H_s
♦   ▲   ★

S_n,   J_s_s,   t_   t_k_
♦   ▲■   ♦   ●▲

_w_y   y__r   s_n.
●●   ♦■   ★

a= ●   e= ▲   i= ★   o= ♦   u= ■

Pray

Thank God for sending His Son Jesus to take away your sin.

Pray

Ask God to help you show love to others

54

WEDNESDAY 1 John 3:17-18

It is not enough to say the <u>words</u> "I love you." You need to do <u>things</u> that show you <u>love</u> others.

Complete the crossword puzzle.
1. _ _ _ _ _ are not enough.
2. You need to do _ _ _ _ _ _
that show you 3. _ _ _ _ others.

Pray
Ask Jesus to help you show love to others.

THURSDAY 1 John 4:1

You need to be careful who you listen to and what you believe. Some people tell lies. The Bible always tells the truth.

Add and use the answers to fill in the blanks.

3 + 1 = _____   1 + 1 = _____

2 + 1 = _____   3 + 2 = _____

2=I; 3=L; 4=B; 5=E

The _ _ _ _ _ is true.
  4 2 4 3 5

Pray
Ask God to help you learn and understand the Bible.

FRIDAY 1 John 4:11

The best way to thank God for loving you is to show love to others.

Look at each picture and ✔ how the children can show love.

Pray
Tell God thank you for loving you.

SATURDAY 1 John 4:21

If you love God, you are commanded to love everyone, including your brothers and sisters.

Circle the pictures of things you can do to show love to others.

Pray
Ask God to help you do loving things for others.

COMMENT CORNER Parent or Leader, circle a comment and/or write your own.

DAYS COMPLETED

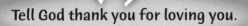
You're special   You can do it   God loves you!   Nice job!   We're proud of you!   Keep it up   WOW!

55

WEEK 20

"Be Healthy"

How can we have healthy bodies and hearts?

Study God's Word and pray each day.

Play outside to get exercise.

Eat good foods.

SUNDAY — 1 John 5:3

How can you show God that you love Him? Obey His Word.

BIBLE

Start at the number 20 and connect the dots to see what you should read and obey.

22
29
23
27
28
32
24

30
21
31
20
26
25

Pray

Ask God to help you obey your parents.

TUESDAY — 1 John 5:21

This is a warning to you. Do not serve anyone or anything but the one true God.

Complete the puzzle to see who you should serve.

U   o   O

en   T   d   er

MONDAY — 1 John 5:14

God <u>hears</u> you when you <u>pray</u>. He will answer according to His will with what is best for you.

Write the correct word that goes with the picture to complete the sentence.

When you _ _ _ _ _ _

God _ _ _ _ _ _ _ you.

Pray

Tell God thank you for hearing your prayers.

Pray

Pray that God will help you keep Him first.

56

WEDNESDAY   2 John 4

John was happy that the children of the church were obeying God's Word.

Circle the picture of the people who should obey God's Word:

Pray

Ask God to help you and your family to obey God's Word.

THURSDAY   2 John 8

When you are obedient to God, you will be rewarded in Heaven.

Have you been faithful to God by obeying Him? If so, write your name on the line of the reward.

FAITHFUL

LOVE, GOD

Pray

Ask Jesus to help you obey Him.

FRIDAY   3 John 2

John wanted the new Christians to have healthy bodies and healthy hearts.

Color the pictures in each group to show the fraction.

$\frac{2}{4}$ 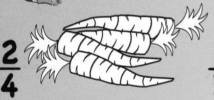 $\frac{1}{5}$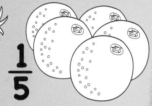

$\frac{1}{3}$  $\frac{1}{2}$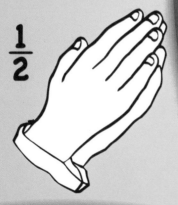

Pray

Tell God thank you for giving you healthy food to eat.

SATURDAY   3 John 11

Do not repeat the bad things others say and do. When you do good things, you show your love for God.

Color the picture of the hands to remind you to pray. Fold your hands, close your eyes and ask God to help you do what is right.

Pray

Ask Jesus to help you do right things.

COMMENT CORNER
Parent or Leader, circle a comment and/or write your own.

You're special   You can do it   God loves you!   Nice job!   We're proud of you!   Keep it up   WOW!

DAYS COMPLETED

WEEK 21

SUNDAY — Ezra 1:2

Trace the rainbow and color it to help you remember to keep your promises.

Red
Orange
Yellow
Green
Blue
Purple

Pray Ask God to help you to keep your promises.

God had promised that His temple would be rebuilt. God always keeps His promises. Can others count on you?

MONDAY — Ezra 2:69

Everybody gave money to rebuild the temple. God helps you so you are able to give to Him.

Count the coins and write the amount.

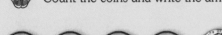

 ¢ _____

 ¢ _____

 ¢ _____

Pray Tell God thank you that you are able to give to Him.

TUESDAY — Ezra 3:3

Even though the Israelites were afraid, they still did right.

Brave is the opposite of afraid. Color the pictures that show you how to be brave.

Pray Ask God to help you when you feel afraid.

WEDNESDAY — Ezra 4:1-2

Adversary is a word for enemy. Your enemy is Satan. He wants you to disobey God.

You need to obey God. Put a star by the ways you can obey God today.

_____ Be kind to others.

_____ Do my quiet time.

_____ Obey my parents.

_____ Clean my room.

_____ Love my brothers/sisters.

Pray
Ask God to help you obey Him.

THURSDAY — Ezra 4:6

Some people will try to stop you from serving God. Don't listen to them.

Find your way through the maze to Jesus, showing you want to serve Him.

GO
STOP
GO
GO
STOP
GO
Start
GO
GO
STOP

Pray
Ask God to help you serve Him today.

FRIDAY — Ezra 4:24

Even though the Israelites were stopped from building the temple, they couldn't be stopped from loving God.

Draw an X over the stop sign. Color the heart red.

STOP

Pray
Thank God for His never ending love.

SATURDAY — Ezra 5:5

God watched over the Israelites and protected them.

God watches over and protects you all the time. Write the time.

___ o'clock ___ : 00

___ o'clock 6 : ___

___ o'clock ___ : 00

Pray
Thank God for always watching over you.

COMMENT CORNER
Parent or Leader, circle a comment and/or write your own.

You're special   You can do it   God loves you!   Nice job!   We're proud of you!   Keep it up   WOW!

DAYS COMPLETED

59

WEEK 22

Ezra 5:11

"Be Wise Guys"

How can you be wise?

By reading God's Word.

Obeying God's Word.

You can be a helper to God, too. Choose one thing you can do today and circle it.

SHARE

HELP A FRIEND

PRAY

SET THE TABLE

Pray
Ask God how you can help today.

TELL SOMEONE ABOUT JESUS

The Israelites were called servants of God. Servants are helpers.

MONDAY

Ezra 6:12

Ezra 6:16

TUESDAY

King Darius made laws and was in charge. God is King, and you should obey His laws.

The Israelites were happy that God's house was finished. Are you happy when you go to church?

Draw an X on the crown shape that fits.

Circle the seven things that are different in the bottom picture.

Pray
Thank God for your church.

Pray
Thank God for the King of kings, Jesus.

WEDNESDAY — Ezra 7:10

Ezra studied God's Word so he could learn how to be obedient to God.

Write every other letter on the lines to see how you can learn to be obedient to God.

A R G D K R O E N A W D L G I O S D D S F W L O

_ _ _ _ , _ _ _ _ _ _

Pray
Thank God for His Word, the Bible.

THURSDAY — Ezra 7:25

God gave Ezra wisdom. He used God's wisdom to teach others about God.

Tell somebody about God today. Write the person's name on the line and color in the star when you've told them.

Pray
Ask God to help you tell your friends about Him.

SATURDAY — Ezra 8:29

The Israelites kept the temple treasures safe. Your treasure is God's Word. You need to keep it in your heart by memorizing verses from it.

Circle the treasure you want in your heart.

Pray
Thank God for the treasure of His Word.

FRIDAY — Ezra 8:23

God hears and answers your prayers.

Cross out all the L's to find out when you can pray. Write the letters in the space.

LLALLNLYLLLTLLLILMLLLEL

_ _ _ _ _ _ _

Pray
Thank God for listening to you when you pray.

COMMENT CORNER

Parent or Leader, circle a comment and/or write your own.

you're special   You can do it   God loves you!   Nice job!   We're proud of you!   Keep it up   WOW!

DAYS COMPLETED

61

WEEK 23

"SIN = SADNESS"

What is sin?

Disobeying.

Not pleasing God.

Doing wrong.

SUNDAY
Ezra 9:3

Sin should make you sad. It keeps you from God. Put a happy face next to things that are pleasing to God, and a sad face next to things that are not pleasing to God.

☺ ☹

○ Obeying God

○ Lying

○ Telling the truth

○ Doing it my way

○ Hating others

○ Loving one another

Pray

Ask God to help you make God happy.

MONDAY
Ezra 9:14

Breaking and forgetting God's commandments lead to sin.

Write the letters in using the code to find what you should not forget.

20=A; 21=C; 22=D; 23=E; 24=G;
25=M; 26=N; 27=O; 28=S; 29=T

—— —— —— ——
24 27 22 28

—— —— —— —— —— —— —— ——
20 26 22 25 23 26 29 28

—— —— —— ——
21 27 25 25

Pray

Ask God to help you obey His commandments.

Ezra was sad over the sins of the Israelites.

TUESDAY
Ezra 10:1

The people were very sad because of their sin. Sin makes God very sad.

Color in the face that shows how God feels when you sin.

Pray

Ask God to help you not to sin.

62

WEDNESDAY
Ezra 10:11

You must confess your sin to make things right with God. He will forgive you when you tell Him that you are sorry.

Follow each numbered ray of light from Jesus to find the letters you need to put in each numbered box.

3
2
6
1
5
8 4 7
O
R
V
I
S
G
E
F

1 2 3 4 5 6 7 8

Pray
Tell God you are sorry for your sin.

THURSDAY
Haggai 1:7

You must consider your way. You should go God's way and not your own way.

Your feet should walk in God's way. Follow the footsteps to find God's way.

Start

God

Pray
Ask God to help you follow Him.

FRIDAY
Haggai 2:4

God wants you to be strong in Him. He can help you.

Color the weights that tell you how you can be strong in the Lord.

Pray.

Go to church.

Read your Bible.

Memorize scripture.

Do my quiet time.

Pray
Ask God to help you grow strong in Him.

SATURDAY
Haggai 2:19

Complete the sentence by writing the first letter of each object in the boxes.

God wants to bless you. Jesus is the best blessing!

God sent

___ ___ ___ ___ ___

Pray
Thank God for giving you Jesus.

COMMENT CORNER
Parent or Leader, circle a comment and/or write your own.

You're special   You can do it   God loves you!   Nice job!   We're proud of you!   Keep it up   WOW!

DAYS COMPLETED

63

WEEK 24

"Life Lessons from Nehemiah

The Bible is full of great stories.

But the stories can also teach us lessons.

One of my favorites is Nehemiah.

Yes, it teaches us about being God's servant, about praying and fasting, about working peacefully and so much more.

SUNDAY
Nehemiah 1:10

Do you see yourself as a servant of God? Nehemiah was willing to do whatever God wanted. Place an X in the box next to pictures that are ways you can serve Him.

Nehemiah saw himself and all the Israelites as servants of God.

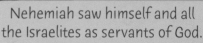

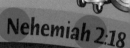

Pray
Pray that you will be a good servant of God.

TUESDAY
Nehemiah 2:18

When Nehemiah arrived in Jerusalem, he shared what God did. It was God who blessed Nehemiah when the king allowed him to travel to Jerusalem and kept him safe. God is in control of everything.

Help Nehemiah get to Jerusalem to repair the wall. Be sure to stop and ask the king's permission.

Jerusalem

MONDAY
Nehemiah 2:4

Before Nehemiah went to the king to ask permission to return to <u>Jerusalem</u>, he spent time praying and fasting. Even as he asked the king's permission he prayed once more to God. You can pray to God anytime, anywhere. You can never pray too much.

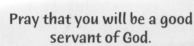

Complete the crossword puzzle.

Across
3. Where did Nehemiah want to go?

Down
1. Nehemiah did this before and while he asked the king.
2. Nehemiah did this before going to the king.

Pray
Ask God to help you to remember to pray whenever you need Him.

Pray
Thank God for something He has done for you.

WEDNESDAY Nehemiah 3:11-13

It took many people working together to rebuild the wall of Jerusalem. It is important to work together peacefully to finish God's work.

Few **Many**

The first column shows a few. Draw many in the second column.

Pray

Ask God to help you get along with others.

THURSDAY Nehemiah 3:28, 32

Priests helped to rebuild the wall, as well as goldsmiths and merchants. Nehemiah was the king's cup bearer, yet he helped to rebuild the wall. Those who helped rebuild the wall had many different jobs. God wants you, no matter what you do, to serve Him, to do His work.

Unscramble the letters to find out what you should do.

_ _ _ _ _ _ _ _

VERSE ODG

Pray

Ask God how you can serve Him today.

SATURDAY Nehemiah 4:14

Nehemiah encouraged the people when they got discouraged and the enemy was frightening them. He reminded them that they served a great and awesome God.

You can encourage someone by cheering them on. Can you think of someone who might need some encouragement to finish a project, or learn something new, or to do their best at something? Make that person a card or poster of encouragement. When you have done that, you may color this ribbon.

I am an encourager!

Pray

Praise God for being great and awesome.

FRIDAY Nehemiah 4:8-9

Some men were angry about the rebuilding of the wall. But this did not stop Nehemiah or the workers. They prayed to God to protect them. While they worked, they kept watch for their enemies.

can be hard and even scary to do things for God, but ke Nehemiah you must not stop. You must pray to God nd keep on working. Cross out the items listed below. he words that are left will tell you what God will do.

Cross out
2 vegetables, 2 insects, 2 sports, 2 animals.

Carrots ladybug **God** baseball **will** cat **protect** broccoli mosquito **soccer you** monkey

Pray

Pray for God to protect you in all that you do.

COMMENT CORNER

Parent or Leader, circle a comment and/or write your own.

You're special You can do it God loves you! Nice job! We're proud of you! Keep it up WOW!

DAYS COMPLETED

65

"Tough Stuff? Stick with God.

Rebuilding the wall was not an easy task. Do you think Nehemiah gave up?

No, he stuck with it.

And they finished the wall in just 52 days.

And then they could rejoice and worship God.

SUNDAY
Nehemiah 5:9

Nehemiah had to correct the people when they were mistreating one another. It is important for you to treat others kindly as an example of God's love for all people.

Complete the puzzle.
Write the letters in the colored boxes on the line.

I need to be ☐ ☐ ☐ ☐.

Pray that today you will practice being kind to everyone.

SINK ☐ICE BANK GO☐D

MONDAY
Nehemiah 6:8-9

There were men who continued to be angry about the rebuilding of the wall. They began to make up lies that Nehemiah wanted to be king. Nehemiah still didn't give in. He kept going, trusting God, and praying for strength to continue the job.

Even if this puzzle is hard for you, don't give up trying. Help Nehemiah continue his work on the wall. Move to a new square that has a number greater than the square you are on. You can also move if the square is half the number of the one you are on. You cannot move diagonally. Watch out for the angry men!

Pray
Ask God to help you trust in Him in difficult times.

start

1	0	1	5	2	5	9
6	3	5	6	3	8	2
2	7	3	2	4	3	5
9	5	4	8	6	6	1
5	6	3	2	1	7	8
3	1	5	6	5	2	1
8	3	9	3	8	4	3
7	4	2	7	6	5	9
6	9	1	5	3	2	1
3	4	8	2	8	4	6

finish

TUESDAY
Nehemiah 6:15-

The rebuilding of this huge wall was completed in only 52 days. Their work showed what an awesome God they served. The things you do can also show people the awesome God you serve.

Fill in the missing numbers to count to 52, the number of days it took to rebuild the wall.

1 2 3 __ 5 6 __ 8 9
10 __ 12 13 14 __ 16
17 __ 19 20 __ 22 __
24 25 __ 27 28 29
__ 31 32 33 __ 35
__ 37 38 39 __ 41
__ 43 __ 45 46 47
48 __ 50 51 __

Pray
Praise God today. Tell Him how awesome He is.

WEDNESDAY — Nehemiah 8:8

When the wall was finished, the people gathered to read God's Word. The priests read the Word and explained the Word so that the people could understand.

When you go to church, you have a teacher who takes time to explain God's Word to you so you can understand. Be thankful for that person. Write a thank you note to your teacher.

Dear
Thank you

Pray
Pray for your pastor, your Sunday school teacher, and your children's church leader. Thank God for all of them.

THURSDAY — Nehemiah 9:2-3

You should model the Israelites. Take time every day to confess your sin, read God's Word, and worship God.

To model someone means to do what they do. Our shadows do what we do. Match the shadows to the correct picture.

Pray
Pray that you will take time every day to do these things.

FRIDAY — Nehemiah 12:42-43

The work was done! God kept His people strong and safe to finish the wall. Choirs sang and the people rejoiced and gave thanks to God.

Can you tell the story of Nehemiah. Number the sentences in order.

— The people rebuilt the wall in Jerusalem.

— The king gave Nehemiah permission to go to Jerusalem.

— The people praised God and read His Word.

Pray
Rejoice and celebrate about something God has done for you.

SATURDAY — Nehemiah 13:13

Nehemiah still obeyed God even after the wall was finished. If people were doing evil in their jobs, Nehemiah would give their job to someone else who would do it right.

Read the sentences. What would you do? Write it down on the lines. Would you have Nehemiah's courage to stop evil?

#1: You see two children teasing another child on the playground. What would you do?

_____
_____

#2: You go to the store with a friend. Your friend takes a pack of gum and puts it in his pocket and starts to walk to the door without paying for it. What would you do?

_____
_____

Pray
Ask God to help you have courage to stop bad things when you see them happening.

COMMENT CORNER
Parent or Leader, circle a comment and/or write your own.

You're special   You can do it   God loves you!   Nice job!   We're proud of you!   Keep it up   WOW!

DAYS COMPLETED

67

"The Holy Spirit"

When a person believes in Jesus to save him, what does God give them?

The Holy Spirit helps us understand God's Word and convicts us when we do something wrong.

The Holy Spirit, but why?

SUNDAY
Acts 1:8

Solve the code to complete the sentence.

Th_ H_ly Sp_r_t
w_ll g_v_ y__
p_w_r t_
w_tn_ss.

E I O U

If you have asked Jesus to forgive your sin, the Holy Spirit will help you tell others about Jesus.

Pray
Ask Jesus to help you tell others you meet about Him.

MONDAY
Acts 1:14

Prayer is very important to Christians. It is the way you can talk to God.

Color the picture of the children talking to God.

Pray
Tell God thank you for listening to your prayers.

TUESDAY
Acts 2:2-4

God gave the Holy Spirit to the believers so they could tell everyone about Jesus.

If you are a Christian, the Holy Spirit will help you. Color the dotted spaces to find where a Christian's power comes from.

HOLY SPIRIT

Pray
Ask God to help you listen to the Holy Spirit.

WEDNESDAY — Acts 2:21

Have you called on Jesus to save you from your sin? Sin is anything you do that disobeys God's rules.

If you have asked Jesus to save you from your sin, color the word YES. If you have not, color the word NO. If you want to know how you can call on Jesus, you can talk to your parents or an adult at church.

YES NO

Pray Thank Jesus for hearing you when you call on Him.

THURSDAY — Acts 2:23-24, 32

Jesus died on the cross to take the punishment for your sin. But He didn't stay dead. He came alive again in three days. At least 500 people saw Jesus after He came back to life. He now lives in Heaven.

Put the pictures in the order that they happened then color the pictures.

Pray Tell Jesus thank you for taking the punishment for your sin.

FRIDAY — Acts 2:46-47

The new Christians met together every day in the temple courts to worship God and learn more about Him. Many other people also came to hear about what Jesus had done for them. They became Christians, too, by asking Jesus to forgive their sin.

Complete the maze to bring all the Christians together to praise God.

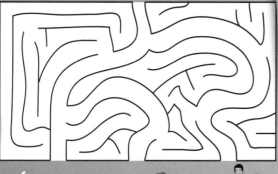

Pray Thank God for your church family.

SATURDAY — Acts 3:6-8

The crippled man wanted money. Peter had something much better than money to give him. Jesus gave Peter the power to heal the man so he could walk. After the man was healed, he was walking, jumping, and praising God.

Peter performed a miracle. God gave him the power through the Holy Spirit to heal this man. Trace the words and then write them on the line.

Pray Tell God thank you for giving you things that you need.

GOD IS POWERFUL

_____

_____

DAYS COMPLETED

"Apostles' Work"

What did the apostles do?

They told others about Jesus.

WE can do that, too!

SUNDAY — Acts 3:19

Follow the lines to figure out what letter belongs on each line.

To be _____, you must tell God that you are _____.

f e r g o v i n

r o s r y

Pray

Tell Jesus thank you for forgiving you when you sin.

God will forgive your sin if you tell Him you are sorry for it. To truly repent you must also stop doing the sin.

MONDAY — Acts 4:12

There is only one way that you can be saved from your sin. You have to ask Jesus to forgive your sin. He is the one and only way for salvation.

Answer the questions.

How many ways are there to be saved?

_____

Who must you believe in to be saved?

_____

TUESDAY — Acts 4:20

Peter and John were excited to tell others about Jesus. They wanted to tell everyone they met what they had seen and heard Jesus do.

Check off places where you can tell others about Jesus.

___ School

___ Doctor's Office

___ Grocery store

___ Playground

___ Church

___ Home

___ Sports gam[e]

Pray

Thank Jesus for dying on the cross and coming alive again to save you from your sin.

Pray

Ask Jesus to help you tell others about Him.

WEDNESDAY — Acts 4:32

All the believers agreed about everything. They never argued with each other. The believers shared everything they owned. You show you <u>care</u> when you <u>share</u>.

Write the missing words in the blanks and then draw a picture of something you can share today.

I show I _ _ _ _ when I _ _ _ _ _.

Pray
Ask Jesus to help you share your toys with your friends.

THURSDAY — Acts 5:3

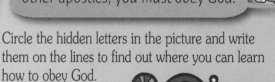

Satan wants you to do wrong. He will try to make you sin today, but God will help you do what is right.

Draw lines from the names Satan and God to the words on the right that tell what each person would want you to do.

Satan   Do what is right

God   Disobey and sin

Pray
Ask God to help you not disobey Him.

FRIDAY — Acts 5:14

Many people wanted to become believers in Jesus because of what Peter and John were teaching about Him.

Many men and women asked Jesus to be their Savior from sin. Add the people.

3 + 1 = ___   2 + 2 = ___

  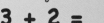

3 + 2 = ___   2 + 1 = ___

Pray
Ask Jesus to help you tell others about Him.

SATURDAY — Acts 5:29

Just like Peter and all the other apostles, you must obey God.

Circle the hidden letters in the picture and write them on the lines to find out where you can learn how to obey God.

_____ _____ _____ _____ _____

Pray
Ask God to help you obey Him.

COMMENT CORNER
Parent or Leader, circle a comment and/or write your own.

You're special   You can do it   God loves you!   Nice job!   We're proud of you!   Keep it up   **WOW!**

DAYS COMPLETED

WEEK 28

"Love One Another"

Who are our brothers and sisters in Christ?

Anyone who is a Christian.

How should we treat them?

With kindness and love.

SUNDAY — Acts 5:42

The apostles told about Jesus every day with those they met and in people's homes.

Complete the maze to remind you to share Jesus with those you meet every day.

Pray
Pray that God will help you talk about Him to others

MONDAY — Acts 6:7

The apostles obeyed God by sharing the Gospel and many believed and were saved. Those who were saved then shared Jesus with others and even more people were saved.

If you tell someone about Jesus, they will want to tell someone else about Him. You can spread the Gospel. Draw a **square** around the 7 things that are different in the bottom picture.

TUESDAY — Acts 7:9-10

God will give you wisdom to say what He wants you to say when you tell others about Him.

Look in a mirror to find the missing word to complete this sentence. Write it on the line.

God will give you _ _ _ _ _ _ when you tell others about Him.

WISDOM

Pray
Ask God to help you know what to say when you tell others about Him.

Pray
Ask Jesus to help you tell a friend about Him today.

72

WEDNESDAY — Acts 7:26

God does not like it when you fight with others. He wants you to be kind and loving especially to other believers.

Circle the right answers.

1. Does God like it when you fight with others? YES or NO

2. God wants you to get along with others. YES or NO

3. It is ok to fight with your brothers/sisters. YES or NO

Pray Ask God to help you be kind to others.

THURSDAY — Acts 7:34

When you pray, God hears you. He is always there for you.

God hears you when you pray. You can pray any time of the day. Put the pictures in 1, 2, 3 order.

Pray Tell God thank you for listening when you pray.

FRIDAY — Acts 7:48-49

God lives in Heaven. Heaven is a beautiful place. If you receive Jesus as your Savior from sin, then one day you will go to live with Him there.

God doesn't live in a house made by a man. Color the picture of the house.

☐ = red.
△ = green.
○ = yellow.
☐ = blue.

Pray Thank God for giving you a home to live in.

SATURDAY — Acts 8:4

The new Christians went everywhere preaching the Good News about Jesus.

You need to tell others everywhere you go about Jesus. Circle the places that you go to where you can tell others about Jesus.

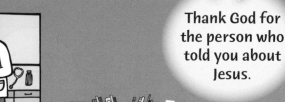

Pray Thank God for the person who told you about Jesus.

COMMENT CORNER
Parent or Leader, circle a comment and/or write your own.

You're special   You can do it   God loves you!   Nice job!   We're proud of you!   Keep it up   WOW!

DAYS COMPLETED

73

"Be a Missionary"

How do you become a missionary?

By simply obeying God and sharing the Gospel.

SUNDAY
Acts 8:25

Peter and John left home to go to Samaria to preach the Gospel. They preached and then returned home.

People all over the world need to hear the Gospel. Follow the lines to find out what you call someone who goes out to preach the Gospel.

Pray
Ask Jesus to help you tell a friend about Him.

MASIONIRSY

MONDAY
Acts 8:36-37

After Philip told the man about Jesus, he wanted to be baptized right away. The man wanted to show that he knew Jesus as his Savior.

If you are saved, have you been baptized to show others that you know Jesus as your Savior? Color the picture of the child being baptized.

Pray
Pray for the pastor at your church.

TUESDAY
Acts 9:4-5

Saul was very mean to Christians. He did not like them, but God changed his heart.

Connect the opposite words to see what changes God can make in a heart.

Sinful Heart	Changed Heart
Hate	Joy
Lie	Kind
Mean	Truth
Unhappy	Love

Pray
Ask God to help you treat others with kindness.

WEDNESDAY — Acts 9:15-16

God chooses ordinary people to tell others about Jesus. You can be a missionary. You don't have to wait until you're grown up.

Draw a line from the children to the blank space. Write the name of someone you want to tell about Jesus.

Pray
Ask Jesus to help you tell someone about Him.

THURSDAY — Acts 9:27

Barnabas stood up for Saul and told about his changed heart.

Find the words in the word search that Barnabas used when he stood up for Saul.

```
X F B L D T
F N T E E E
H V X K H P
G Y N X C P
N H F V A N
M W M G E E
Q F E O R E
N E K O P S
```

PREACHED   SEEN   SPOKEN

Pray
Pray for someone who needs a friend.

FRIDAY — Acts 9:40

Dorcas helped those in need. When she died, everyone was sad. God gave Peter the power to bring Dorcas back to life. Many people believed in Jesus because of this miracle.

Complete the dot to dot then color the picture.

Pray
Pray for someone you know who is sick.

SATURDAY — Acts 10:7-8

An angel of God told Cornelius to send for Peter. Cornelius didn't know why, but he obeyed. God used Cornelius and Peter to tell the people the Good News of Jesus.

You should obey God in all things, even if you don't understand. Draw a square around the 7 things in the bottom picture that are different.

Pray
Ask God to help you obey Him no matter what.

COMMENT CORNER
Parent or Leader, circle a comment and/or write your own.

You're special   You can do it   God loves you!   Nice job!   We're proud of you!   Keep it up   WOW!

DAYS COMPLETED

"The Gospel"

Who should be telling others about Jesus and His salvation?

Me!

Me!

SUNDAY — Acts 10:15

God spoke directly to Peter. God told him it was good to include meat in his meals.

God wants you to eat healthy food.

Everyone had fruit.

Mom and Alex had juice.

Dad had milk.

Mom had a salad.

Dad and Alex had a taco.

	milk	juice	fruit	salad	taco
Dad					
Mom					
Alex					

Pray

Thank God for making all kinds of good food for you to eat.

MONDAY — Acts 10:28

God wants the Gospel message to go to all people, not just a few special ones.

Connect the dots to see with whom you should share the Gospel.

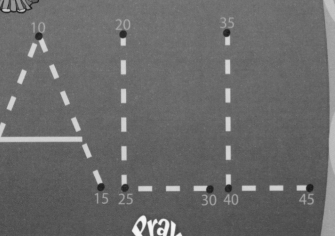

10   20   35

5   15   25   30   40   45

Pray

Ask God to help you tell all people about His Son, Jesus.

TUESDAY — Acts 10:34

Peter said God does not have favorites. He loves everyone just the same.

Underline whom God loves.

Pray

Praise God for His love.

WEDNESDAY   Acts 11:1

The Good News about Jesus dying and coming to life again so our sin could be forgiven was spreading around the world.

Cross out pictures to show the equation. Write how many are left.

3-1=___

Pray

Tell Jesus thank you for coming to be the Savior for everyone, including you.

4-3=___   4-2=___

THURSDAY   Acts 11:21

The Christians told others how Jesus died on the cross and came back to life again. Many people heard the Good News and had their sin forgiven.

You can tell others the Good News, too. Draw a circle around the 6 hidden Bibles.

Pray

Ask Jesus to help you tell a friend about Him.

FRIDAY   Acts 12:9-11

Peter was in jail for telling others about Jesus. God sent an angel to get Peter out of jail so he could keep spreading the news about Jesus.

Draw a line to take Peter out of jail.

Pray

Tell Jesus thank you that you are free to tell others about Him.

SATURDAY   Acts 12:12-14

Many believers were praying for Peter while he was in prison. God heard and answered their prayers.

Do you get excited when God does great things in your life? Color the picture of Rhoda.

Pray

Praise God for two great things He has done for you.

COMMENT CORNER   Parent or Leader, circle a comment and/or write your own.   DAYS COMPLETED

You're special   You can do it   God loves you!   Nice job!   We're proud of you!   Keep it up   WOW!

77

"Light to all the World"

SUNDAY
Acts 13:4-5

Complete the crossword puzzle with the names of the three men who took the Gospel to another place.

Let's sing "This Little Light of Mine" to help us remember to share Christ with others.

Paul, Barnabas and John Mark went to Cyprus (an island) to preach the Gospel.

Pray
Ask Jesus to help you tell others about Him.

MONDAY
Acts 13:25

John the Baptist told the people that Jesus was going to come. God used John to tell others about Him even though he was an ordinary person.

Follow the path from John the Baptist to the village. Every time you come to a circle, copy the letter into the box.

Pray
Ask God to use you to tell others about Jesus even though you are an ordinary person.

TUESDAY
Acts 13:38-39

If you believe in Jesus and what He did for you on the cross, you can have your sin forgiven.

If you know Jesus as your Savior, cross out the SIN in this space and thank God for His Son, Jesus.

SIN

If you do not know Jesus as your Savior, talk to your parents or an adult at church.

Pray
Thank Jesus for dying on the cross to pay for your sin.

WEDNESDAY — Acts 13:47

By telling others about Jesus and His salvation, Christians are a "light" for God.

Color the candle to remind you to be a light by telling others about Christ.

Pray

Ask Jesus to help you tell others about Him.

THURSDAY — Acts 14:8-10

The man had been crippled since birth. He believed that God could heal his legs. Paul was given power by God to heal the man.

Put the pictures in 1, 2, 3 order.

Pray

Pray for someone you know who is sick.

FRIDAY — Acts 14:21-22

Paul and Barnabas were the very first missionaries. Missionaries are people who tell others about Jesus.

You can be a missionary in your own town. Circle the places where you can tell others about Jesus.

Playground
Store
School
Library
Home

Pray

Ask God to help you be a missionary.

SATURDAY — Acts 15:4

The church in Jerusalem welcomed Paul and Barnabas. They shared the wonderful news of all that had happened to the people in the church.

Do you share with others what God is doing in your life? Write or draw one thing that God has done and then check off who you will tell.

___ Sister
___ Brother
___ Mom
___ Dad
___ Teacher
___ Grandma
___ Grandpa
___ Friend
___ Neighbor

Pray

Ask God to help you share the good things He does for you with others.

COMMENT CORNER

Parent or Leader, circle a comment and/or write your own.

You're special
You can do it
God loves you!
Nice job!
We're proud of you!
Keep it up
WOW!

DAYS COMPLETED

WEEK 32

What can we do with the Bible?

Teach others how to be saved.

Learn about Jesus.

Read it daily to get to know God better.

SUNDAY
Acts 15:27

Write the name or draw a picture of your Bible teacher.

God has given the Bible to believers to know how to live. He has also given teachers to explain the Bible to Christians.

Pray

Tell God thank you for your teachers at church.

MONDAY
Acts 15:35

Paul and Barnabas continued to teach other people about the Bible.

Sing this song to remind you what you should share with others.

The B-I-B-L-E,
Yes, that's the Book for me.
I'll read His Word and then obey,
The B-I-B-L-E. Bible!

Pray

Tell God thank you for all of your teachers at church.

TUESDAY
Acts 16:5

Paul faithfully taught about Jesus. Many people were saved and many believers learned more about Jesus. Do you tell others about Jesus?

Find the sums of the numbers in each row. Look at the last number in each row. Write the letter from the code box to find out whom you should be telling others about.

7	8	9	10	11	12	13
R	T	E	J	S	U	F

1	2	1	4	4
+3	+1	+1	+2	+3
+2	+3	+5	+2	+3
+4	+3	+4	+4	+1

____ ____ ____ ____ ____

Pray

Ask Jesus to help you tell someone about Him

WEDNESDAY Acts 16:14

Lydia listened to Paul preach, and God helped her to understand His Word.

You use your ears to listen. Draw a circle around the 6 hidden ears.

Pray Ask God to help you listen to His Word.

THURSDAY Acts 16:25-26

Paul and Silas were in jail for doing God's work, but they were praising God anyway. God caused an earthquake and set them free.

Circle the red letters and write them on the blanks to find out what you should do when things are tough.

SJTPFHRDU
HAIAKUSJE
JSJSDFGEJ
FGSTFYOJD
HDUH

_ _ _ _ _

Pray Ask God to help you when you are in trouble or afraid.

FRIDAY Acts 17:3

Paul taught that Jesus <u>died</u> and <u>rose</u> again to be your <u>Savior</u> from sin.

Unscramble the words to finish the sentence.

Jesus _____ (edid)

and _____ (sero)

again to be your

_____ (rovSai)

Pray Thank God for sending Jesus to be your Savior.

SATURDAY Acts 17:11

The Christians at Berea studied to learn from God's Word.

What did the Christians at Berea study? Connect the dots to find out.

6
20
8 16 18
10
BIBLE
22 4
24
14 2
12

Pray Ask God to help you understand the Bible.

COMMENT CORNER
Parent or Leader, circle a comment and/or write your own.

You're special   You can do it   God loves you!   Nice job!   We're proud of you!   Keep it up   WOW!

DAYS COMPLETED

"The Bible"

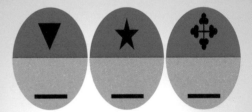

What are some things we learned about the Bible?

It is powerful!

We need to be brave and share it with others.

The Bible is God's plan book for us.

SUNDAY
Acts 17:26

Draw a picture of the home that God gave to you.

God created you! He knew exactly what family you would be in and where you would live.

Pray

Tell God thank you for your home.

MONDAY
Acts 18:9-10

God gave Paul protection so that he could share the Gospel without being hurt.

Find these words.

GOD   GOSPEL   PAUL   PROTECT

```
Y Y L H K T
E M E U H C
U W P Y A E
D I S J M T
M O O Y V O
E L G A Y R
E Q L U A P
```

Pray

Ask Jesus to help you tell others about Him.

TUESDAY
Acts 18:21

Paul wanted to obey God's plan. You should obey God's plan, also.

Use the code to find out where God's plan is.

B E H I L T

Pray

Ask God to help you obey His Word.

WEDNESDAY   Acts 19:8

God gave Paul boldness to teach others about Jesus.

Boldness is not being afraid to tell others about Jesus. Circle the picture of the child showing boldness.

Pray Ask God to help you not be afraid to tell others about Jesus.

THURSDAY   Acts 19:20

God's Word spread to many people. They saw its power and turned away from their sin.

Copy the letters along each path into the boxes to see what is powerful.

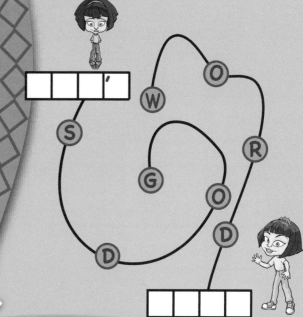

Pray Tell God thank you for His powerful Word.

FRIDAY   Acts 19:29

People were mad at Paul and his friends for sharing the Gospel. But Paul and his friends were brave and continued to teach God's Word.

Check Yes or No after each statement.

Yes   No

1. God wants you to teach His Word. ☐ ☐

2. You should always make fun of others. ☐ ☐

3. You should be brave and tell the Gospel. ☐ ☐

Pray Ask God to help you be brave enough to tell others about Him.

SATURDAY   Acts 20:9-10

God used Paul to do a miracle. He raised the boy from the dead!

Number the pictures in the order that they happened in the story.

Pray Tell God thank you for doing miracles.

COMMENT CORNER
Parent or Leader, circle a comment and/or write your own.

You're special   You can do it   God loves you!   Nice job!   We're proud of you!   Keep it up   **WOW!**

DAYS COMPLETED

WEEK 34

"A Missionary Journey"

Some people were angry at him.

They even tried to kill him.

Paul made journeys far away from his home to tell others about Jesus.

But he kept on preaching!

Color in all the squares that have the letters J and P. Copy the leftover letters, from top to bottom onto the lines.

```
      T
    E   J
  J   P   L
P   L   J   O
P   T   H   J   P
P   E   J   R   J   S
```

Pray
Ask God to help you tell someone about Jesus this week.

_ _ _ _ _

_ _ _ _ _ _ _ _

Paul was a great missionary. He joyfully shared the Good News of Jesus with everyone he met. You can be a missionary right where you are!

Paul worked hard with his hands. He told the people it was much better to give than to receive. Do you share cheerfully with others?

In the open hands write or draw something you can give to others. Giving doesn't always have to be money or things. You can give your time and work, too!

Pray
Ask God to help you give to others cheerfully.

Paul was going to Jerusalem to preach, even though he knew he would be arrested. He was obedient to God, no matter what. Are you obedient even when it's hard?

Draw ropes on Paul's hands and feet to show that he would be arrested for sharing the Gospel. Color the picture.

Pray
Ask God to help you do your best today.

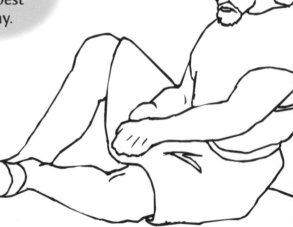

WEDNESDAY — Acts 21:17

The Christians in Jerusalem were friendly to Paul when he arrived. You need to be friendly to new kids who come to your school, neighborhood, and church. They should see Jesus in you.

I will be
_____.

o p d t f a r t i p e t n n d u l a y r o

Start at the arrow and write every other letter on the lines.

Pray Ask God to help you be friendly to others.

THURSDAY — Acts 21:33-36

Paul was beaten and arrested because he preached about Jesus. Through it all, he kept sharing the Good News about Jesus. How do you act when others are unkind to you?

These children are treating others kindly. Under each picture, write an action word from the box.

climb dig slide jump

_____ _____

_____

Pray Pray that God will help you be kind to someone who is not nice to you.

FRIDAY — Acts 22:14-15

If you know Jesus as your Savior, you have been chosen to share Him with others.

Who can you tell about Jesus this week? Circle the 6 things in the bottom picture that are different.

Pray Pray for someone who needs to know Jesus.

SATURDAY — Acts 22:29-30

Paul was a citizen of Rome. This meant he had to be treated fairly by Roman law. God protected Paul and gave him more opportunities to tell people about Jesus.

Find the words in the puzzle.

CITIZEN PAUL ROME

N K H W Q M H
C I T I Z E N
L U A P R I F
S X H R O M E

Pray Ask God to keep you and your family safe.

COMMENT CORNER

Parent or Leader, circle a comment and/or write your own.

You're special   You can do it   God loves you!   Nice job!   We're proud of you!   Keep it up   WOW!

DAYS COMPLETED

"Paul on Trial"

Why would Paul get in trouble when he didn't do anything wrong?

God used it so even more people would hear about Jesus.

The people didn't want to hear about Jesus.

But why wou God let t happen.

SUNDAY — Acts 23:1

Paul obeyed God and was not ashamed of doing His work.

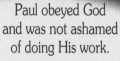

O – B – E –Y
spells the word
"Obey"
Do each thing that
God commands
Read His word and
pray.

Sing the words to the tune of, "Row, Row, Row Your Boat" and answer the question.

Pray
Ask God to help you tell others about Jesus.

How can you obey today?_____

MONDAY — Acts 23:20-21

These people wanted to hurt Paul because he preached about Jesus. Are you willing to tell others about Jesus? Maybe not everyone will listen, but you must obey God.

Find and circle the seven hidden ears in the picture.

Pray
Ask Jesus to help you tell others about Him.

TUESDAY — Acts 23:33-35

Paul was taken safely to the governor with a letter telling about his case. He would be able to preach again God can turn a bad situation into something good.

Match the opposite words.

Sad

Good

Bad

Light

Glad

Dark

Pray
Ask God to help you smile even when things aren't going your way.

WEDNESDAY — Acts 24:15-16

Have you put your hope in God? The only way to have your sin forgiven is to ask Jesus to be your Savior. If you have never done that, ask your parents or an adult at church to tell you how.

If you have asked Jesus to be your Savior, write your name in the Bible. If you haven't, color the Bible, but wait to write your name in it.

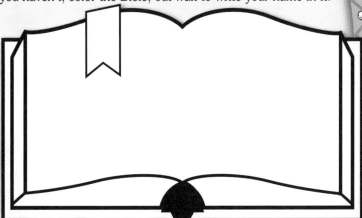

Pray

Thank Jesus for dying on the cross and coming back to life again.

THURSDAY — Acts 24:23

Paul was in prison, but God provided for him. Paul's friends brought him all the things he needed. They took care of him. You should treat your friends kindly, especially those in need.

Circle some of the things Paul's friends might have brought to him in prison.

Pray

Thank God for taking care of you.

FRIDAY — Acts 25:11-12

Paul asked to meet the ruler of Rome. Now he could tell the ruler of Rome about Jesus. That's amazing!

Fill in the vowels to find out what you should do (just like Paul).

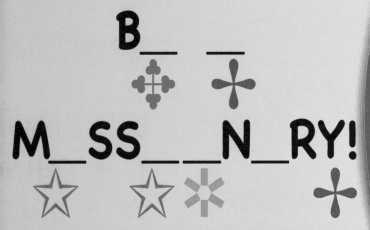

B _ _
M _ SS _ _ _ N _ RY!

✛ +A   ✜ =E   ☆ =I   ✱ =O

Pray

Pray for someone in your neighborhood who needs to know Jesus.

SATURDAY — Acts 25:25

Paul had been in prison for a long time. Still they could not find anything that he had done wrong. Paul continued to trust God. His way is always best!

Complete the puzzle to find the hidden message.

STURT

_ _ _ _ _ _ _ _ _

ODG

Pray

Ask God to help you trust Him.

87

"What Would Jesus Do?"

Not all the time.

Do you stop and think before you speak or act?

You should! You need to make sure you act like Jesus!

Remember WWJD.

SUNDAY — Acts 26:13-15

Complete the maze to take Paul to Damascus.

Paul used to be mean and hurt Christians. One day he saw a bright light from Heaven, and Jesus spoke to Paul and his life was changed forever.

Pray

Ask God to help you show kindness.

MONDAY — Acts 26:19-20

Paul obeyed Jesus by taking the Gospel to both the Jews and the Gentiles.

Draw a line to connect the letter with the word it stands for to help you remember to obey.

W   W   J   D

Jesus   What

Would

Do

Pray

Ask God to help you act like Jesus.

TUESDAY — Acts 27:6-7

Paul was sailing on a long journey to Rome. It was a hard trip, but Paul trusted God to take care of him.

Follow the color key to complete the picture.

B - Brown
Y - Yellow
W - Blue

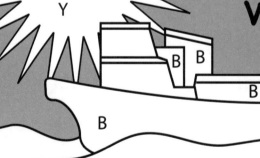

Pray

Pray for people who are traveling today.

WEDNESDAY Acts 27:20, 24-25

A terrible storm almost sunk the ship. God told Paul that no one would be harmed. God was in control of the storm and seas.

Write the letter in the blank that comes before the letter beneath to decode the message.

"With God There Is

___ ___ ___ ___ ___ ___!"
O P   G F B S

Pray

Thank God for watching over you.

THURSDAY Acts 27:42-44

The ship ran into a sandbar and was broken to pieces. God protected Paul and everyone on board. They all swam or floated to shore.

Find the words in the puzzle.
FLOAT   SHORE   SWIM

Q M I W S
B B C H Z
T A O L F
X R E B N
E F K C K

Pray

Pray for the safety of your family.

FRIDAY Acts 28:2

Paul and the others landed on an island called Malta. The people there helped them. You should help those in need, too.

Write or draw something you can do to help someone today.

Pray Pray that God will show you someone who needs your help today.

SATURDAY Acts 28:23-24

It is not enough that your parents or teachers believe in Jesus. You have to choose for yourself. Do you believe in Jesus?

Find all the hidden crosses in the picture to remind you what Jesus did for you.

Pray Ask Jesus to help you tell others about Him.

COMMENT CORNER Parent or Leader, circle a comment and/or write your own.

You're special   You can do it   God loves you!   Nice job!   We're proud of you!   Keep it up   WOW!

DAYS COMPLETED

89

"1, 2, 3..."

Moses wrote the Book of Numbers.

He had to count all of the Israelites.

That was a lot of counting!

SUNDAY
Numbers 1:1

Add the pictures and write your answer on the blank.

$3 + 1 = \_$ $1 + 1 = \_$

$2 + 2 = \_$ $1 + 3 = \_$

God told Moses to count all of the Israelites. You are important and count to God.

Pray

Thank God that you are important to Him.

MONDAY Numbers 1:52

The Israelites lived in tents in the desert. The desert was not their lasting home. The earth is not your forever home. If Jesus is your Savior your real home is Heaven.

Color where your real home is.

Heaven

TUESDAY
Numbers 3:6

The Levites served Aaron the High Priest. You are to be like the Levites and serve Jesus, your High Priest.

Draw a heart by the things you can do to serve.

Set the table.

Make my bed.

Bring a friend to church.

Pray for others.

Share with others.

Pray

Ask Jesus to make you a helper today.

Pray

Thank God for your home in Heaven.

WEDNESDAY — Numbers 3:45

God said the Levites were His. If Jesus is your Savior, you belong to God.

By the way you act, people will see if you belong to God. What do you want people to see? Fill in the heart with God or You.

God
You

Pray

Ask God to help others see that you belong to Him.

THURSDAY — Numbers 6:25

When you please God, He makes His face to shine on you. He will be happy.

Obedience is one way to please God. Cross out the numbers to find out what pleases God.

12O34B56E78D9I24E68N12C345E67

_____

Pray

Ask God to help you make Him happy.

SATURDAY — Numbers 8:11

The Levites were chosen by God to do His work. You can serve God, too.

Complete the puzzle to see what you can do for God.

__ __ __ __ __ __   __ __ __

EREVS GDO

Pray

Ask God to help you tell someone about Jesus.

FRIDAY — Numbers 7:89

Moses heard and listened to the voice of God. You need to listen to His Word and obey Him.

Find these words in the puzzle.

GOD   LISTEN   OBEY

X H F O Y A
L I S T E N
E D J Z B D
E O X D O R
O U D G W M
S O N D D K

Pray

Ask God to help you to be a good listener.

COMMENT CORNER

Parent or Leader, circle a comment and/or write your own.

You're special   You can do it   God loves you!   Nice job!   We're proud of you!   Keep it up   WOW!

DAYS COMPLETED

91

"Grumble"

The Israelites complained about the manna.

They were ungrateful.

We need to be thankful to God.

SUNDAY
Numbers 8:19

Write who you want to be a gift to then color the picture.

1=Green
2=Blue

The Levites helped in the tabernacle. They were like gifts to the priests. You can be a gift to others.

Pray

Ask God to show you who you can help today.

MONDAY
Numbers 9:16

The cloud was a symbol of God's presence. You can know that God is always near.

Circle Yes or No to answer the questions.

Yes   No
You have to be in church for God to be near you.

No
God is near you when you play.
Yes

Pray

Thank God for always being near.

God is near you when you pray.
Yes   No

TUESDAY
Numbers 10:35

Moses prayed for protection from enemies. God wants to protect you from His enemy, Satan.

Write the first letter of each picture to see who will help protect you.

Pray

Thank God for His protection.

WEDNESDAY — Numbers 11:4

The Israelites were complaining again. They were tired of manna and wanted meat. They were ungrateful for God's provision.

Don't be like the Israelites. Be grateful! Read the sentences. Write each action word.

I _ _ _ _ my Bible.

I _ _ _ _ with my friends.

I _ _ to church with my family.

My mommy _ _ _ _ _ good food.

I _ _ _ my clothes away.

read play go cooks put

Pray
Tell God thank you for what He gives you.

THURSDAY — Numbers 11:33

God punished the Israelites for not being content and trusting that He knew best.

Use the key to write the missing vowel to find out when you should trust the Lord.

_ll th_ t_m_.
1   2   3 2

1=A   2=E   3=I

Pray
Ask God to help you trust Him.

FRIDAY — Numbers 12:1-2

Miriam was jealous of Moses. She said unkind things about him to others.

Fill your mouth with kind words by drawing lines from the words to the mouth. Is your mouth pleasing to God?

I hate you.

Let me help you.

_d is good.

Excuse me.

I am not your friend anymore.

Pray
Ask God to help you say kind words to others.

SATURDAY — Numbers 13:3

Moses sent 12 men to spy out the Promised Land. Heaven is your promised land if you believe in Jesus.

There is only one way to Heaven; believing that Jesus died on the cross for your sin. Find your way through the maze. Remember, only one way!

Start

Heaven

Pray
Thank God for Heaven.

WEEK 39

"Promised Land"

Caleb and Joshua got to go to the Promised Land.

They trusted in God.

The Promised Land is a picture of Heaven.

God wants you to trust Him. Put a star by the best answer to finish the question. As a Christian you should…

☐ not listen to God's Word.

☐ listen to God's Word.

☐ listen and trust in God's Word.

Pray
Ask God to help you listen to Him.

10 men gave a bad report about the Promised Land. 2 men gave a good report of the Promised Land. The Israelites listened to the 10 men instead of trusting God.

MONDAY   Numbers 14:18

TUESDAY   Numbers 14:24

God is <u>patient</u>, <u>forgiving</u>, and full of <u>mercy</u>. God wants you to be the same.

Because Caleb trusted in God, he was allowed into the Promised Land. If you trust in Jesus as your Savior from sin, you will be allowed into Heaven.

Find the underlined words in the word search.

If you asked Jesus to forgive your sin, you will see Him in Heaven someday. Color the picture of Heaven as a reminder of this promise. If you aren't sure you will go to Heaven someday, talk your parent or a teacher at church.

T	F	K	P	L
N	O	I	K	D
E	R	O	C	W
I	G	M	Q	K
T	I	E	N	V
A	V	R	E	S
P	P	R	Z	O
Z	N	Y	R	M
G	G	M	Q	M

Pray
Ask God to help you follow and obey Him.

Pray
Ask God to help you be patient and not impatient.

94

WEDNESDAY — Numbers 14:45

The Israelites tried to fight the battle on their own and lost. They did not want God's help. When you do things on your own strength, you will fail.

Who should you ask for help when you are in trouble? To find the answer, cross out the numbers and write the letters on the lines.

1 9 3 3 4 3
G 3 9 4
8 8 2 8
2 4 D 7
9 2 7 O 1 1

Pray
Ask God to help you be strong in Him.

___ ___ ___

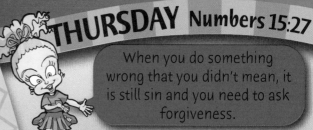

THURSDAY — Numbers 15:27

When you do something wrong that you didn't mean, it is still sin and you need to ask forgiveness.

You just can't be sorry with your mouth. You have to mean it in your heart. Draw a ☐ around the child who is really sorry.

Pray
Thank God that He forgives you when you ask.

FRIDAY — Numbers 17:8

Aaron's dead branch bloomed and had fruit! Just like the branch, Jesus was also dead but came alive again.

Start at the arrow and write every other letter on the lines.

Start

E I P O J P E
G O
V S
F I
I U
S Q
L S
L A E S W I U

___ ___ ___ ___ ___ ___
    ___ ___
___ ___ ___ ___ ___ .

Pray
Thank God that Jesus is alive.

SATURDAY — Numbers 20:12

God told Moses to speak to the rock. He disobeyed God and spoke to the people and hit the rock. Moses did it his way and sinned.

Disobeying is sin. Find the word sin hidden in the picture. Put an X on it. Underline the word that tells you what you should say to sin.

Pray
Ask God to help you obey.

NO
YES

COMMENT CORNER
Parent or Leader, circle a comment and/or write your own.

You're special   You can do it   God loves you!   Nice job!   We're proud of you!   Keep it up   WOW!

DAYS COMPLETED

"Follow the Leader"

Moses' job of leading the people is almost done.

Moses was a good follower of God.

I want to be like Moses and follow God.

SUNDAY — Numbers 21:6, 8

God sent snakes to bite the Israelites. To be healed, they had to look up at a bronze snake on a pole.

Complete the dot to dot to see how Jesus died for your sin.

60
70
90
80
50
40
100
20
30
10

Pray

Thank Jesus for dying for your sin.

MONDAY — Numbers 22:12

God said that the Israelites are blessed. You are special to God.

Who should you thank for making you special? Trace the heart around the answer when you have said thank you.

_ _ _ _

Pray

Thank God for making you special.

TUESDAY — Numbers 22:28

God used a donkey to teach Balaam to obey Him.

God wants you to obey Him. If you are a child of God, you will obey Him. Complete the dot to dot to remind you what you need to

K
J
H
G
I
L
10
15
B   C   5
D
20
30
E
25
35
A
F
40
50   N
45
55
8
7
60
6
1
5   2
4   3

Pray

Ask God to help you obey Him.

WEDNESDAY — Numbers 27:16-17

You are like a sheep without a shepherd. Jesus came to be your shepherd and to lead and protect you.

Draw a line from the sheep to the words that have the long e sound like the word sheep.

Sheep

Tree

Egg

Pray

Thank Jesus for being your Shepherd.

Leaf

3 Three

THURSDAY — Numbers 32:15

Moses gave a warning about not turning away from God. You are to follow God.

When you turn away from following God, you usually end up going your way. Find the best path for your life.

MY WAY **GOD'S WAY**

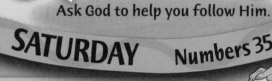

Pray

Ask God to help you follow Him.

FRIDAY — Numbers 32:23

Your sin will find you out. You can't hide your sin from God.

When you try to hide your sin it makes things worse. Find the hidden letters of the word sin and circle them. Then write the letters on the praying hands to remind you not to hide your sin, but to ask forgiveness for your sin.

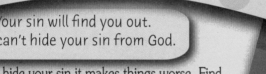

Pray

Ask God to help you do right even when on one is looking.

SATURDAY — Numbers 35:13

The Israelites had cities of refuge. Refuge means safety. God is your refuge. He will take care of you.

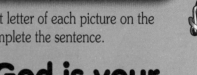

Write the first letter of each picture on the blanks to complete the sentence.

God is your

_____ _____ _____ _____ _____

Pray

Thank God for His safety.

COMMENT CORNER

Parent or Leader, circle a comment and/or write your own.

You're special   **You can do it**   **God loves you!**   **Nice job!**   **We're proud of you!**   **Keep it up**   **WOW!**

DAYS COMPLETED

WEEK 41

"The Gospel Message"

How would you describe the Gospel?

The Good News.

God's plan to save us.

A gift from God.

SUNDAY
Galatians 1:3-4

Write the name or draw a picture of someone you can tell this week about God's love.

_____

Jesus died for your sin because God, His Father, asked Him to do so. He did this because He loves you.

Pray

Thank God for sending Jesus to die for you.

MONDAY
Galatians 1:10

You should try to please God in all you do.

Draw a circle around the 5 hidden Bibles in the picture.

Pray

Ask God to help you please Him today.

TUESDAY
Galatians 1:20

God knows <u>everything</u>. You can't hide your sin from Him. Lying is wrong and doesn't please God. You should always tell the <u>truth</u>.

Finish the sentences and fill in the crossword puzzle.

Across
2. God knows

Down
1. Always tell the

Pray

Ask God to help you always tell the truth.

WEDNESDAY — Galatians 2:2

Paul and his friend, Barnabas, shared the Gospel everywhere they went. God wants you to share the Good News with others, even with people you do not know.

Connect the words in the first column to the Bible verses in the second column to help you know what to share with others.

Gift	Romans 10:13
Believe	Romans 6:23
Call	Romans 10:9

Pray
Ask God to help you tell someone the Good News today.

THURSDAY — Galatians 2:12-13

Peter was trying to please people instead of God. Paul told him he needed to try to please Jesus no matter who was watching. You need to obey Jesus even when nobody will see you.

Follow the lines to fill in the blanks to finish the sentence.

You need to

_ _ _ _   _ _ _ _ _.

y o b e   e s u J s

Pray
Thank God for always watching over you.

FRIDAY — Galatians 2:16

Doing good works does not get you to Heaven. Believing in Jesus as your Savior from sin does. You should always do good to please God.

Draw a triangle around the 6 things in the bottom picture that are different.

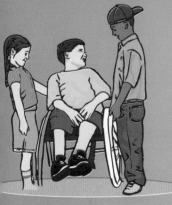

Pray
Ask Jesus to help you please Him.

SATURDAY — Galatians 3:2-3

It is your belief in Jesus that saves you from your sin. If you are saved, only Jesus can help you do what is right. You cannot do it alone.

Color the arrow that shows the way to be saved from your sin.

GOOD DEEDS

BELIEVE IN JESUS

Pray
Ask God to help you follow Him.

COMMENT CORNER
Parent or Leader, circle a comment and/or write your own.

You're special   You can do it   God loves you!   Nice job!   We're proud of you!   Keep it up   WOW!

DAYS COMPLETED

WEEK 42

SUNDAY
Galatians 3:13-14

"Inheritance"

When we believe in Christ and what He has done for us, we become sons of God. What have we seen fathers give to their heirs (sons) in the Bible?

Blessings.

All that the family owned.

The responsibility of caring for the family.

Complete the dot to dot.

60 70
90
80
50
40
100
20
30
10

Jesus died on the cross for you. He did it to set you free from sin. He wants to forgive you.

Pray
Tell Jesus thank you for setting you free from your sin.

MONDAY
Galatians 3:22

Believing that Jesus died for your sin is the only way to find forgiveness for the wrong things you do.

Doing good things will not erase the bad things you have done. Only Jesus can take away your sin. Circle yes or no to answer the question.

Have you ever asked Jesus to forgive your sin?
YES NO

If you are not sure, talk to your parents or teacher at church.

Pray
Ask Jesus to help you obey Him.

TUESDAY
Galatians 3:26

If you have asked Jesus to forgive your sin, you are a child of God. You are a special part of God's family.

Complete the maze to find out how to join God's family.

Your Name

JESUS

Family of God

Pray
Pray for each member of your family

100

WEDNESDAY — Galatians 4:6

When you ask Jesus to be your Savior, He gives you His Holy Spirit as a gift. The Holy Spirit will always be with you. He helps you obey God's Word.

Jesus is the best gift you could ever receive. Color and decorate the present. Write your name on the tag.

to:
from: GOD

Pray — Tell God thank you for His gift to you.

THURSDAY — Galatians 4:13-14

The people took care of Paul even though it was difficult for them to do so. Jesus wants you to be kind to others no matter what they may be like.

Circle the pictures showing how Jesus wants you to treat others.

Pray — Pray for someone who is sick.

FRIDAY — Galatians 4:22-23

God promised Abraham and Sarah that He would give them a son. They were very old, but God gave them Isaac. Nothing is too hard for God. He always keeps His promises.

Fill in the blanks with the first letter of each picture to complete the sentence.

God always keeps His

_ _ _ _ _ _ _ _

Pray — Tell God thank you for always keeping His promises.

SATURDAY — Galatians 5:1

Jesus paid the price to set you free from sin.

CHRIST   FREE   STAND

I	S	T	A	N	D
Q	W	S	V	K	Y
L	F	I	W	F	Z
C	R	R	N	B	I
Y	C	H	E	F	G
I	Y	C	F	E	V

Find and circle the words in the puzzle.

Pray — Ask God to help you say no to sin.

COMMENT CORNER

Parent or Leader, circle a comment and/or write your own.

You're special   You can do it   God loves you!   Nice job!   We're proud of you!   Keep it up   WOW!

DAYS COMPLETED

WEEK 43

"Do to Others..."

God cares about how we treat all people.

Yeah, people will see we're Christians by our actions.

Especially how we treat other Christians.

SUNDAY
Galatians 5:6

Color the picture to remind you of Jesus' love for you.

LOVE

Pray

The way you love shows others that you know Jesus. You can show people you know Jesus by the way you treat your family and friends.

Ask God to help you show His love to others.

MONDAY
Galatians 5:14

To love your neighbor according to God's command is to do for them what you would do for yourself.

Cross out the numbers in the puzzle to show God's instructions.

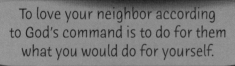

5L86O4V3E36Y86O29U1R165
47N2E97I33G2H26B53O28R4
1A63S9Y33O3U2R74S9E5L2F7

_ _ _ _   _ _ _ _ _

_ _ _ _ _ _ _ _ _

_ _   _ _ _ _ _ _ _

Pray

Pray for someone who is unkind to you.

TUESDAY
Galatians 5:16

Ask God for His help to keep you from doing wrong. His Spirit will help you know what is right to do.

Draw a line to finish each sentence.

The Spirit

will go away from what is right

You alone

will help you do what is right.

Pray

Ask Jesus to help you have good actions in your life.

102

WEDNESDAY — Galatians 5:22-23

When you trust Jesus as your Savior, the Holy Spirit comes to live within you. Others can see that you love Jesus by the way you act – your fruit.

Color all the fruit of the Spirit that others should see in you.

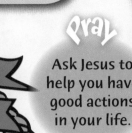

Pray
Ask Jesus to help you have good actions in your life.

Fruit basket labels: self-control, joy, patience, meekness, peace, gentleness, love, faith, goodness

THURSDAY — Galatians 6:2

Jesus has commanded believers to help each other (bear one another's burdens).

Write the number of a way to "help" next to the burden it can help.

BURDENS	HELPS
___ Hungry	1. Give a coat.
___ Cold	2. Share a meal.
___ Sick	3. Pray for healing.

Pray
Ask Jesus to make you a helper in your neighborhood.

FRIDAY — Galatians 6:9-10

Do not get tired of doing what is right. Keep doing what God wants you to do. He will reward you when the time is right.

Using the key, color the letters to remind you what to do.

DO GOOD

1 = Red
2 = Pink
3 = Purple

Pray
Ask Jesus to help you not get tired of doing good.

SATURDAY — Galatians 6:14

Do not be proud of what you can do—give all the praise to Jesus who has done so much for you.

a, e, i, o, u

Write the correct vowel in the blank.

G_v_ _ll

pr_ _ s _

t_

J_ s _ s.

Pray
Praise Jesus for loving you so much.

COMMENT CORNER

Parent or Leader, circle a comment and/or write your own.

You're special
You can do it
God loves you!
Nice job!
We're proud of you!
Keep it up
WOW!

DAYS COMPLETED

103

WEEK 44

"Wise Words"

God told King Solomon He would give him anything he wanted.

It was written by King Solomon.

What do you know of the Book of Proverbs?

Solomon asked God to give him wisdom.

Some of that wisdom is written down in the Book of Proverbs.

SUNDAY — Proverbs 11:1

Circle the scales that are being honest.

God hates dishonesty. You are dishonest when you cheat at a game or when you tell a lie. It pleases God when you are honest and truthful.

Pray Ask God to help you be honest in all things.

MONDAY — Proverbs 11:17

When you are kind to others, you feel good and God is pleased. When you are mean to others, you feel bad and God is sad.

Draw a line from each word on the left to its opposite on the right.

Mean	Obey
Bad	Honesty
Dishonest	Happy
Sad	Kind
Disobey	Good

Pray Ask God to help you be kind.

TUESDAY — Proverbs 11:23

Jesus will return someday. If you believe Jesus died for your sin, you can look forward to this time with happiness. Those who don't believe only have God's anger over their sin to look forward to.

Complete the crossword puzzle.

Anger
Believe
Will
End

Across
3. Those who don't believe will have to face God's _____ for their sins.
4. Jesus _____ return someday.

Down
1. The world will _____.
2. Those who _____ have nothing to fear.

Pray Pray that people will believe Jesus is the Savior before He returns.

WEDNESDAY — Proverbs 12:1

In order to learn, you have to be taught and sometimes corrected. Correction isn't fun, but it is necessary to help us learn. God calls the person who hates correction a fool.

Have you ever thanked your parents for correcting you, for taking time to show you right from wrong? The Bible tells us in Proverbs 3:12 that parents correct their children because they love them, just as God does. Thank your parents for correcting and showing you love. Finish this Thank You note for your parent.

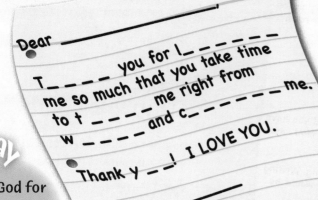

Dear _____

T_____ you for l_ _ _ _ _ _ me so much that you take time to t_ _ _ _ me right from _____ and c_ _ _ _ _ _ me. w_ _ _ _ and c_ _ _ _ _ _ me.

Thank y_ _! I LOVE YOU.

thank; loving; teach; wrong; correct; you.

Pray

Thank God for your parents who love you and correct you.

THURSDAY — Proverbs 12:15

The wise way is God's way. It pleases Him. Wise people listen to others. Fools don't listen to others because they think they already know everything.

Be wise! Listen to your parents, to teachers, and to other grown ups who love God. Follow the words that rhyme with ear to take the children to their parents.

ear
hear
near
cheer
tear

Pray

Ask God to help you use your ears for listening.

FRIDAY — Proverbs 12:22

God hates when you tell lies. He is happy when you tell the truth.

Color all the bricks in the pyramid that have the letters J, P, and S. Copy the leftover letters from top to bottom onto the lines.

I should

_ _ _ _ _ _ _ _ _ _ _
_ _ _ _ _ _ _ _ _

```
        T
      E   J
    S   P   L
  L   P   T   J
 H   P   S   E   J
T   S   J   R   S   P
J   U   P   J   T   S   H
```

Pray

Ask God to help you always tell the truth even when it is hard.

SATURDAY — Proverbs 13:10

Pride can cause you to argue with others because you think you are right. When you listen to others, you will often learn something and gain wisdom.

Use the word bank to fill in the blanks.

Be quick to h_____,

slow to s_____,

slow to a_____.

hear
speak
anger

Pray

Pray James 1:19. Ask God to help you be quick to hear, slow to speak, and slow to anger.

COMMENT CORNER

Parent or Leader, circle a comment and/or write your own.

You're special   You can do it   God loves you!   Nice job!   We're proud of you!   Keep it up   WOW!

DAYS COMPLETED

"Wisdom or Foolishness

Proverbs compares the way of the foolish with the way of wise.

A foolish person thinks sin is funny.

A wise person shows love to everyone.

A wise person thinks before they act.

A foolish person doesn't listen to teaching.

SUNDAY

A wise person thinks before he acts. A foolish person does not think. He shows he is unwise by his actions.

Check the wise choice.

1. You were tossing a ball in the living room. It hit a picture sitting on top on the table, which then fell down and broke. Mom comes into the room and sees the broken picture. Do you...

☐ Tell her your brother knocked it over.

☐ Say that you were tossing a ball and broke it. You know you will be punished.

2. You forgot to study for your spelling test. Mom and Dad said you have to do well on this test or no more baseball after school. Your friend says you can look at her paper if you get stuck. Do you...

☐ stop and think. Looking at her paper would be cheating. Writing down answers that are not yours would be lying. You would be sinning. You are not going to do that.

☐ It's okay. You're only going to look if you get stuck and need a clue. You will never do it again. No one will know. You will study next time.

Proverbs 13:16

Pray

Ask God to help you stop and think and be wise when you act.

MONDAY

Proverbs 14:9

Sin is never funny or something to brag about. When you sin, you should feel bad and seek forgiveness from God and the person you hurt.

Hidden in this pile of X's is a message. Write the letters on the lines to find the message.

XXXXFXXXXOXXXOXXXLXXXS
XXFXXXIXXXNXXXXXXXXDXX
SXXXXXXXIXXXXXXXNXXXXX
XFXXXUXXXNXXXXXNXXXXXY

‾ ‾ ‾ ‾ ‾ ‾ ‾ ‾ ‾ ‾ ‾ ‾

‾ ‾ ‾ ‾ ‾ ‾ ‾ ‾ .

Pray

Have you hurt somebody? Ask their forgiveness. Ask God for forgiveness and pray for the person.

TUESDAY

Proverbs 14:21

Is there someone you dislike or even hate? The Bible tells you that is a sin. The wise way, God's way, is to love your neighbors and your enemies.

Bible Treasure Hunt: Use these clues to discover where in the Bible God tells us to love our neighbors and our enemies.

Clue 1: It is a New Testament book.

Clue 2: It is one of the gospels.

Clue 3: It starts with the letter before N.

Clue 4: It is the longer name.

Clue 5: It is in Chapter 11 + 11 =

Clue 6: It is verse 40 − 1 =.

‾‾‾‾‾‾‾‾‾‾‾‾‾‾‾ ‾‾‾:‾‾‾

Pray

Ask God to help you to love those you don't like.

WEDNESDAY — Proverbs 14:35

God is your eternal King. You are to be His servant. When you do what is good and right, He is happy and rejoices. When you do what is wrong, He is angry.

The way of the wise makes God happy. The way of the fool makes God angry. Count by fives and write the numbers.

Pray

Praise the King of kings. Pray that you will be a good servant.

THURSDAY — Proverbs 15:3

God sees and knows everything. He sees all that is good. He sees all that is bad. He sees everything you do.

God sees everything. What do you see? Color one box for each child.

 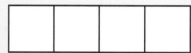

 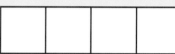

Pray

Pray that you will please God in all that you do.

FRIDAY — Proverbs 15:20

If you have been faithful in doing your quiet time the past two weeks, you have learned some of what God says is wise and what is foolish. God tells us that a wise child will make his father glad.

Make your Father in Heaven glad, make wise choices, and follow what you have learned from the Bible. Color the picture of Jesus. Give Him a happy face if you have been doing what is wise.

Pray

Thank God for His Word and the things you have learned.

SATURDAY — Proverbs 15:24

If you have asked Jesus to be your Savior, the Holy Spirit will help you to make wise choices and walk the path of the righteous. This path ends in Heaven.

Color the path you want to follow.

HEAVEN

- Be giving.
- Be truthful.
- Steal.
- Love your neighbors and enemies.
- Lie.
- Sin is bad.
- Just do it.
- Believe in Jesus.
- Don't believe in God.

Pray

Thank God for the Holy Spirit who is your helper in hard times.

COMMENT CORNER

Parent or Leader, circle a comment and/or write your own.

You're special   You can do it   God loves you!   Nice job!   We're proud of you!   Keep it up   WOW!

DAYS COMPLETED

WEEK 46

"Educators and Encouragers"

God is so good to us.

He gives us grown-ups to learn from.

And He gives us Christian friends to encourage us.

SUNDAY
1 Thessalonians 1:2

You should thank God for the people He has put in your life. Check off three people to pray for today.

__Mom __Dad

__Teacher __Pastor

__Friend __Relative

__Sister/Brother

__Missionary

Paul prayed for the Christians in the city of Thessalonica.

Pray
Tell God thank you for your friends.

MONDAY
1 Thessalonians 1:8

The believers in Thessalonica were busy spreading God's Word and sharing their faith.

If you ask Jesus to be your Savior from sin, you need to tell others. Write the first letter of each picture on the lines to complete the sentence.

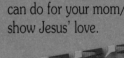

Pray
Ask God to help you be a good listener of His Word, the Bible.

Pray
Ask Jesus to help you tell a friend about Him.

TUESDAY
1 Thessalonians 2:

Not only is it important to share the Gospel with others, it is important to do things for others.

Write or draw one thing you can do for your mom/dad to show Jesus' love.

WEDNESDAY 1 Thessalonians 2:13

The Christians listened to God's Word and did what He said.

Put a star by the best answer to finish the sentence.

As a Christian you should. . .

___ not listen to God's Word.

___ listen to God's Word.

___ listen and obey God's Word.

Pray Ask God to help you be a better listener.

THURSDAY 1 Thessalonians 2:20

The Thessalonians' obedience to God gave Paul and Timothy joy. Paul and Timothy loved to see people obey God.

Write the vowels into the blanks to see what you should do.

AEIOU

When others see you _b_y G_d you br_ng them j_y.

Pray Tell God thank you for people in your life who love and obey Him.

FRIDAY 1 Thessalonians 3:2

Because Paul could not be with these believers, he sent Timothy to help and encourage them.

Write the name of someone who helps you follow God. Make a card to say thank you and give it to him/her this week.

Pray Tell God thank you for your teachers at church.

SATURDAY 1 Thessalonians 3:12

If you are a Christian you should have more and more love for others as you grow in God.

Add these numbers to give you the code of what you should do.

1 +2 =E	8 +9 =H	10 +5 =L	3 +3 =O
5 +4 =R	2 +2 =S	7 +6 =T	5 +5 =V

15	6	10	3		6	13	17	3	9	4

Pray Ask God to help you show love to others.

COMMENT CORNER

Parent or Leader, circle a comment and/or write your own.

You're special   You can do it   God loves you!   Nice job!   We're proud of you!   Keep it up   WOW!

DAYS COMPLETED

109

WEEK 47

The Bible tells us how to be ready when Jesus calls all His believers home to Heaven.

SUNDAY
1 Thessalonians 4:1

Hold your quiet time book up to a mirror to reveal the message.

To please God, you need to OBEY Him even MORE.

Pray
Ask God to help you obey Him.

As you learn more about God's Word, you need to live more like Jesus.

MONDAY
1 Thessalonians 4:9

Loving one another is very important to God

Write the letters inside the red hearts to see what God wants you to do.

T L O V E I C
O N E S Y T R
A N O T H E R

_____ _____ _____

_____ _____ _____

Pray
Ask God to help you show love to others.

TUESDAY
1 Thessalonians 4:16-17

One day Jesus will come back with a shout and a trumpet sound. He will take to Heaven all those who believe in Him. The dead will go first and then those who are living.

Write your answers in the boxes.

Do you believe in Jesus?

Will you go to heaven forever?

Pray
Tell Jesus thank you for caring enough to take you to Heaven someday.

Wednesday — 1 Thessalonians 5:2

No one knows when or what time Jesus will call Christians home to Heaven to be with Him.

If you are ready to go to Heaven, you should be sharing the Gospel with others so they may know Jesus and be ready, too. Write the name of somebody you can share the Gospel with inside the heart.

Pray
Ask Jesus to help you tell others about Him.

THURSDAY — 1 Thessalonians 5:13

You need to live at peace with everyone.

You should not argue or fight. Color 6 hidden crosses in the picture.

Pray
Ask God to help you live at peace with everyone.

FRIDAY — 1 Thessalonians 5:17

You can talk to God about everything all the time!

Write the time.

____ : ____

____ : ____

____ : ____

Pray
Tell God thank you for always listening.

SATURDAY — 1 Thessalonians 5:24

God is faithful. He will keep His promises. God will love and care for you forever.

Complete the first part of the verse and then fill in the crossword puzzle.

1. F __ __ __ __ __ __ __
is 2. __ __ who
3. c __ __ __ __ __ you.

Pray
Tell God thank you for being faithful.

DAYS COMPLETED

COMMENT CORNER
Parent or Leader, circle a comment and/or write your own.

You're special   You can do it   God loves you!   Nice job!   We're proud of you!   Keep it up   WOW!

111

WEEK 48

"Growing Faith"

How can we grow in faith?

God wants you to continue to grow and build up your faith.

By reading the Bible

And doing what it says.

2 Thessalonians 1:3

Use the code to fill in the blanks to answer the question.

A=10; E=20; F=30; H=40; I=50;
L=60; O=70; T=80; V=90

What two things should you be growing in?

1. __ __ __ __ __
   30 10 50 80 40

2. __ __ __ __.
   60 70 90 20

God wants you to continue to grow in your faith and your love for one another just like the Christians in Thessalonica.

Pray
Ask God to help you learn more about Him.

MONDAY

2 Thessalonians 1:10

If you believed Jesus saved you from your sin, the things you say and do should bring glory to God.

Fill in a happy face by the things that bring glory to God and a sad face by the things that do not glorify God.

Read your Bible and pray.
⚪

Fight with your brother/sister.
⚪

Share your favorite toy.
⚪

Tell someone about Jesus' love.
⚪

Pray
Ask Jesus to help you bring glory to Him.

TUESDAY

2 Thessalonians 2

These believers were being taught untrue things and Paul wrote to tell them the truth.

Follow the lines to complete the sentence.

Remember: God's Word is

__ __ __ __ __.

T U H T R

Pray
Thank Jesus for your Bible.

112

WEDNESDAY — 2 Thessalonians

One day everyone who does not believe in Jesus will be punished by God.

Jesus died on a cross and came to life again to take the punishment for your sin. Jesus loves you very much. Color the picture.

Pray

Thank Jesus for dying on the cross for your sin.

THURSDAY — 2 Thessalonians 2:13

If you are a Christian, you have been chosen by God.

Find the words in the word search: chosen, salvation, belief

```
I C S A D P
U Q A H S I
W J L K Q X
S H V J F V
U Q A Z E J
I Q T D I O
A Y I I L Y
C H O S E N
E E N X B S
```

Pray

Thank God for your friends who believe in Jesus.

FRIDAY — 2 Thessalonians 3:3

God has promised to keep His children safe and protect them from the evil one.

Fill in the vowels to complete this promise from the Bible.

A, I, O, U

G___D is
F___ __THF__L!

Pray

Tell Jesus thank you for keeping you safe.

SATURDAY — 2 Thessalonians 3:13

Paul encouraged the Christians not to get tired of doing good things that pleased God.

Color the heart by things you can do to please God.

Obey my parents.

Read and obey the Bible.

Share my toys.

Tell the truth.

Pray

Ask God to help you do things that please Him.

COMMENT CORNER

Parent or Leader, circle a comment or write your own.

You're special   You can do it   God loves you!   Nice job!   We're proud of you!   Keep it up   WOW!

DAYS COMPLETED

WEEK 49

"Bearing Fruit"

Yum! I love fruit.

Not the kind you eat.

In the Bible we are told that we need to bear fruit.

No, this fruit is called the Fruit of the Spirit!

SUNDAY
Colossians 1:4-6

Color the good grapes **purple** and the bad grapes **brown**.

- Gentleness
- Love
- Stealing
- Kindness
- Peace
- Joy
- Disobeying
- Lying

If you are a follower of Jesus, you should bear fruit, not grapes or apples, but the Fruit of the Spirit. Things like love and kindness should show in your life.

Pray

Ask God to help you show love and kindness in your life.

MONDAY
Colossians 1:10-11

Don't keep your love for Jesus a secret. Let it show by the way you talk and act. Everyone should be able to tell that you know Jesus.

Find the five pieces of hidden fruit in the picture and circle each one.

Pray

Ask Jesus to help others know that you love Him.

TUESDAY Colossian 1:15-16

Jesus is not only the Son of God – He is God! He created everything! You were created by Him and for Him.

Draw a picture of yourself. You are God's special creation.

Pray

Thank God for creating you just as you are.

WEDNESDAY — Colossian 1:22

Sin separates you from God. If you ask Jesus to forgive your sin, He brings you close to God.

Skip count by fives to see what Jesus has done for you to bring you back to God.

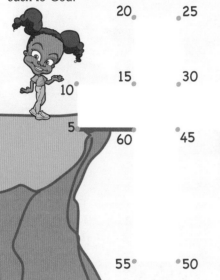

20   25

15   30   35

10

5   GOD

60   45   40

55   50

Thank God for His Son Jesus.

Pray

THURSDAY — Colossians 1:24

Paul was happy that the people were learning about Jesus. He was praising God that so many people were going to church.

Start at the arrow. Write every other letter on the blanks to find another name for the church.

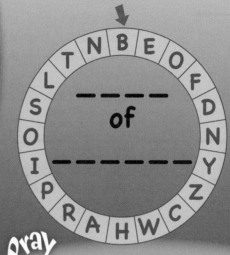

_ _ _ _
of
_ _ _ _ _ _

Pray

Tell God thank you for your church.

FRIDAY — Colossians 2:6-7

Do you regularly thank God and others? Being thankful for everything is a good way of showing that you know Jesus. You can be thankful for so much.

Draw something you are thankful for today.

Pray

Thank God for your family.

SATURDAY — Colossians 2:10

Jesus is all you need. Toys, things, and friends can never make you happy or content like Jesus can.

This picture of fruit is incomplete, just like you are without Jesus. Draw the other half to finish the picture.

Pray

Ask Jesus to give you a happy heart today.

COMMENT CORNER

Parent or Leader, circle a comment or write your own.

You're special   You can do it   God loves you!   Nice job!   We're proud of you!   Keep it up

DAYS COMPLETED

WOW!

115

"Tame the Tongue"

SUNDAY
Colossians 2:16-17

Write the first letter of each word to complete the phrase.

Your relationship with God is what really matters.

Pray

Ask Jesus to help you please Him today.

MONDAY
Colossians 3:2

You need to be careful not to love all the things you have. You need to think on things that really matter. Things that matter are people, the Bible, and obeying God.

Circle the pictures of things that matter to God.

Pray

Ask God to help you keep Him first before all other things.

TUESDAY Colossians 3:8-10

You need to get rid of words that are wrong (sinful). Use good, kind words instead of bad language.

Draw lines from the mouth to the good words. Cross out the things you should not say with your mouth.

Lies　　**Prayer**

Singing　　**Gossip**

Arguing　　**Praise**

Kindness

Pray

Ask God to help you speak with truth and kindness.

WEDNESDAY — Colossians 3:20

When you obey your parents, you please God. Obeying is doing what you are told the first time with a happy heart.

Write or draw some way you can obey your parents today.

PRAY

Ask God to help you obey first time with a happy heart.

THURSDAY — Colossians 4:6

You need to be very careful to say only what is true, kind, and helpful. That way people will be able to see Jesus in you.

Under each picture write an action word from the box.

climb dig slide jump

_____   _____

_____

Pray

Ask God to help you speak kindly to others.

FRIDAY — Colossians 4:7-8

Paul had special friends who helped him share the Good News. He needed them to care for him in prison and take messages to others.

Cross out every other letter and fill in the blanks to see what you can do to be a helper at church.
The first letter is crossed out for you.

P O R H A J Y G W S O Y R Z K U G B I L V Q E

P _ _ _

W _ _ _

G _ _ _

Pray

Ask Jesus to help you be a helper at your church.

SATURDAY — Colossians 4:17

When you are given a job, you should do it. Don't wait! Remember you are doing it to please God not yourself. Do everything the very best you can!

Draw a picture that completes the sentence.

Today, I will do my best when . . .

Pray

Ask God to help you do your best when you are given a job.

COMMENT CORNER

Parent or Leader, circle a comment and/or write your own.

You're special   You can do it   God loves you!   Nice job!   We're proud of you!   Keep it up   WOW!

DAYS COMPLETED

117

"Growing Up"

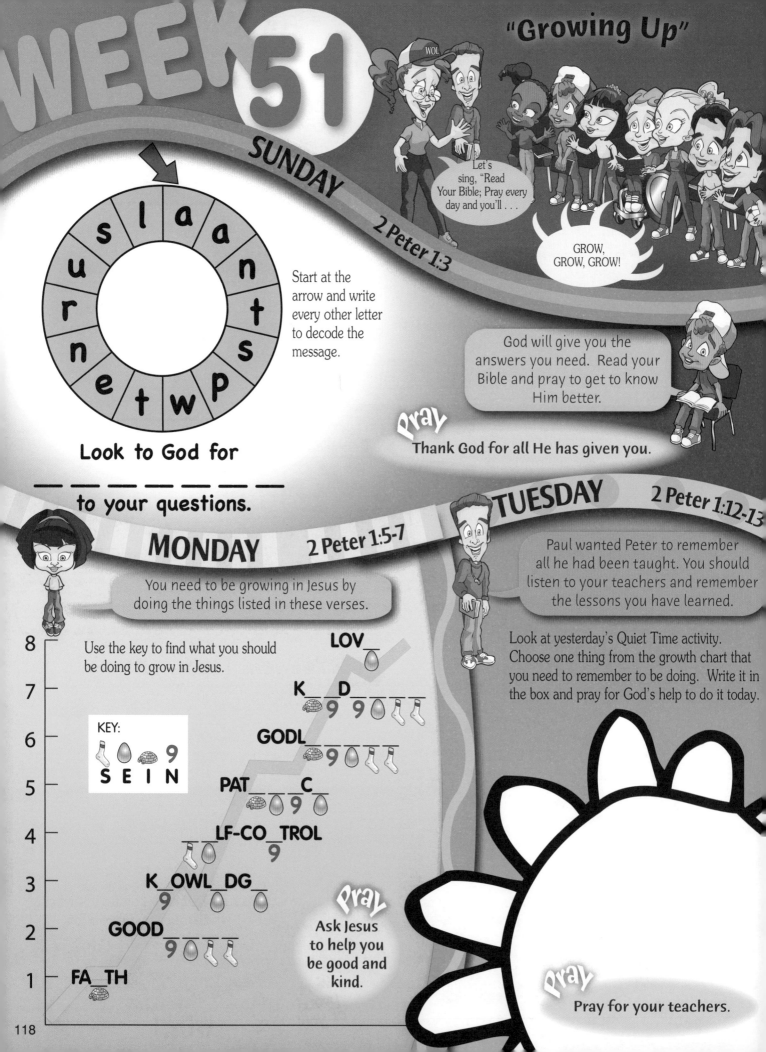

SUNDAY — 2 Peter 1:3

Start at the arrow and write every other letter to decode the message.

Look to God for

_ _ _ _ _ _ _

to your questions.

Let's sing, "Read Your Bible; Pray every day and you'll . . .

GROW, GROW, GROW!

God will give you the answers you need. Read your Bible and pray to get to know Him better.

Pray
Thank God for all He has given you.

MONDAY — 2 Peter 1:5-7

You need to be growing in Jesus by doing the things listed in these verses.

Use the key to find what you should be doing to grow in Jesus.

KEY:
S E I N

8 LOV_
7 K_ _D _ _ _ _
6 GODL_ _ _ _ _
5 PAT_ _ _ C_
4 _ _ LF-CO_TROL
3 K_ OWL_ DG_
2 GOOD_ _ _ _
1 FA_ TH

Pray
Ask Jesus to help you be good and kind.

TUESDAY — 2 Peter 1:12-13

Paul wanted Peter to remember all he had been taught. You should listen to your teachers and remember the lessons you have learned.

Look at yesterday's Quiet Time activity. Choose one thing from the growth chart that you need to remember to be doing. Write it in the box and pray for God's help to do it today.

Pray
Pray for your teachers.

WEDNESDAY
2 Peter 1:16-17

Peter heard God say that He loved Jesus and was pleased with Him.

God loves you, too! Circle two things you can do to please Him today.

LISTEN IN SCHOOL.
OBEY PARENTS FIRST TIME.
CLEAN UP ROOM.
SHARE TOYS.
PRAY FOR MISSIONARIES.
MEMORIZE A VERSE.

Pray
Tell God thank you for sending Jesus to save you from your sin.

THURSDAY
2 Peter 2:9

God will protect the obedient, but He will punish the wicked.

Follow each numbered line to find the letter you need to put in the numbered circle.

3 2 6 1 4 7 5 B E O G Y D O

1 2 3 4 5 6 7

Pray
Ask God to help you obey Him.

FRIDAY
2 Peter 2:12

Those who do not preach the truth will be punished by God.

Unscramble the letters to answer the questions.

1. What do you need to know?
T _ _ _ _ H (TUR)

2. Where can you find the truth?
B _ B _ _ _ (LEI)

3. Who can help you know the truth? G _ D (O)

Pray
Praise God for all the beautiful things He has made.

SATURDAY
2 Peter 2:21

When you hear God's Word, it is important to obey it.

Complete the maze. Pick up the letters—write them in order—read what you should do with God's Word.

Start

I T E Y O B

Finish

Pray
Ask God to help you obey His Word.

_ _ _ _ _ _ _

COMMENT CORNER
Parent or Leader, circle a comment and/or write your own.

You're special
You can do it
God loves you!
Nice job!
We're proud of you!
Keep it up
WOW!

DAYS COMPLETED

WEEK 52

God shows us truth through His Word. How can we know the truth?

Reading the Bible.

Memorizing Bible verses.

Listening to our Bible teachers.

SUNDAY
2 Peter 3:5

God made you. Draw a picture of YOU in the mirror and thank God for creating you.

Remember that God made the world and all that is in it. He only had to speak and all was created.

Pray

Thank God for making you special.

MONDAY
2 Peter 3:9

Jesus doesn't want anyone to be separated from Him. He wants everyone to be saved from their sin. Jesus died on a cross to save you from your sin.

Count by tens and complete the dot to dot.

★ 10

100   20   30

90   80   50   40

70   60

Pray

Pray for a friend or family member who doesn't know Jesus.

TUESDAY
2 Peter 3:18

You grow in knowledge of the Lord by reading His Word and learning His truths. You bring Him glory by knowing Him better.

Color the flowers that tell how you can grow in the Lord.

PRAY

DO YOUR QUIET TIME

READ THE BIBLE

GO TO CHURCH

MEMORIZE BIBLE VERSES

Pray

Ask God to help you listen to His Word so you can grow in Him.

WEDNESDAY — Jude 3

Jude wanted his friends to tell others about Jesus. Do you know how to tell others about Jesus?

Draw a line to match the verse to the truth!

1. Romans 6:23

2. John 3:16

3. Acts 16:31

Believe on the Lord Jesus Christ

God sent His Son

Pray

Ask Jesus to help you tell others about Him.

THURSDAY — Jude 8

Some people who do not believe in God do not respect authority.

Put an X by the people that God has put in charge of you that you must respect and obey.

___ Mother

___ Father

___ Teacher

___ Pastor

___ Coach

___ Grandmother

___ Grandfather

Pray

Pray for someone you know who does not believe in God.

FRIDAY — Jude 16

Don't grumble and complain. There is so much for which you can be thankful. Let your words be kind and sweet. This pleases God.

Fill the missing letters in to remind you what words you should be using.

k_nd

sw__t

Pray

Ask God to help you use kind words.

Pray

Ask Jesus to help you be like Him.

SATURDAY — Jude 21

To help you stay in the Truth and know God, it is good to be with other believers.

Do you have a good friend who loves God and helps you do what is right? Put that friend's name in the heart and color the heart your friend's favorite color.

COMMENT CORNER
Parent or Leader, circle a comment and/or wri...

You're special

You can do it

God loves you!

Nice job!

We're proud of you!

Keep it up

WOW!

DAYS COMPLETED

121

"A True Friend"

Ruth's name means friendship.

She was a good friend to Naomi.

Ruth was a good friend of God, too.

SUNDAY — Ruth 1:8

God is pleased when you help others. Circle the pictures of things you can do to show kindness to others.

Naomi was very sad. Orpah and Ruth were kind to Naomi and tried to make her feel better.

Pray
Ask God to help you be kind to someone today.

MONDAY — Ruth 1:16

Ruth wanted to know Naomi's God. Do others want to know about your God?

Don't keep your love for God a secret. Find the three letters hidden in the picture and write them on the line.

G O D

____ ____ ____

Pray
Ask God to help you tell others about Him.

TUESDAY — Ruth 2:2

Ruth was a hard worker. God is pleased when you work hard, and He rewards hard work.

1. Make my bed
2. Clean my room
3. Take out the trash
4. Wash the dishes
5. Visit someone who is sick
6. Make a card for someone

Choose 2 things you can do for God. Write the numbers in the sheaves of grain. Remember to do them!

Pray
Ask God to help you work hard today.

WEDNESDAY — Ruth 2:16

Boaz took care of Ruth and her needs. Jesus loves you and will take care of your needs.

Circle the words in the puzzle.

CHURCH   CLOTHES   FOOD   HOME   PARENTS

```
R A L V E S K
H T Y A K E D
Q C E M O H U
P A R E N T S
Z I S U T O Q
Y K B O H L Q
F O O D Z C W
```

Pray

Thank Jesus for caring for you.

THURSDAY — Ruth 3:5

Ruth listened to and obeyed Naomi. When you listen and obey, you please God.

Follow the hearts that lead to God.

Start

Listen · Obey · Listen · Obey · Listen · Obey · Listen · Listen · Obey · Obey

God

Pray

Ask God to help you to listen and obey today.

FRIDAY — Ruth 4:9

Boaz redeemed Ruth. That means he paid the price so that Ruth could be in his family. Jesus redeemed you by dying on the cross and paying the price for your sin.

Circle the picture showing how Jesus paid the price. Write Thank You Jesus.

_____

Pray Thank Jesus for paying the price for your sin.

SATURDAY — Ruth 4:13

Ruth now had a new family. When you become God's child, you belong to God's family. You become His son or daughter.

Color the picture of the boy and girl who are the son and daughter of God. If you are a son of God, circle the boy, if you are a daughter of God, circle the girl.

Pray

Thank God for your family.

COMMENT CORNER

Parent or Leader, circle a comment and/or write your own.

You're special   You can do it   God loves you!   Nice job!   We're proud of you!   Keep it up   WOW!

DAYS COMPLETED

To Word of Life Club Members

So that all club and family members will be on the same passages, the following dates correspond to the weekly passages. These dates are used for all Word of Life Quiet Times and daily radio broadcasts.

Week 1	Aug 24 – Aug 30	Psalms 51:1-56:13	Week 28	Mar 1 – Mar 7	Acts 5:33-8:13
Week 2	Aug 31 – Sep 6	Psalms 57:1-63:11	Week 29	Mar 8 – Mar 14	Acts 8:14-10:8
Week 3	Sep 7 – Sep 13	Psalms 64:1-68:35	Week 30	Mar 15 – Mar 21	Acts 10:9-12:25
Week 4	Sep 14 – Sep 20	Psalms 69:1-72:11	Week 31	Mar 22 – Mar 28	Acts 13:1-15:12
Week 5	Sep 21 – Sep 27	Psalms 72:12-76:12	Week 32	Mar 29 – Apr 4	Acts 15:13-17:21
Week 6	Sep 28 – Oct 4	1 Timothy 1:1-4:8	Week 33	Apr 5 – Apr 11	Acts 17:22-20:12
Week 7	Oct 5 – Oct 11	1 Timothy 4:9-6:21	Week 34	Apr 12 – Apr 18	Acts 20:13-22:30
Week 8	Oct 12 – Oct 18	Leviticus 1:1-23:14	Week 35	Apr 19 – Apr 25	Acts 23:1-25:27
Week 9	Oct 19 – Oct 25	Leviticus 23:15-26:46	Week 36	Apr 26 – May 2	Acts 26:1-28:31
Week 10	Oct 26 – Nov 1	Mark 1:1-3:12	Week 37	May 3 – May 9	Numbers 1:1-8:18
Week 11	Nov 2 – Nov 8	Mark 3:13-5:20	Week 38	May 10 – May 16	Numbers 8:19-13:25
Week 12	Nov 9 – Nov 15	Mark 5:21-7:13	Week 39	May 17 – May 23	Numbers 13:26-20:12
Week 13	Nov 16 – Nov 22	Mark 7:14-9:29	Week 40	May 24 – May 30	Numbers 20:23-35:25
Week 14	Nov 23 – Nov 29	Mark 9:30-11:11	Week 41	May 31 – Jun 6	Galatians 1:1-3:9
Week 15	Nov 30 – Dec 6	Mark 11:12-13:23	Week 42	Jun 7 – Jun 13	Galatians 3:10-5:1
Week 16	Dec 7 – Dec 13	Mark 13:24-14:65	Week 43	Jun 14 – Jun 20	Galatians 5:2-6:18
Week 17	Dec 14 – Dec 20	Mark 14:66-16:20	Week 44	Jun 21 – Jun 27	Proverbs 11:1-13:13
Week 18	Dec 21 – Dec 27	1 John 1:1-2:27	Week 45	Jun 28 – Jul 4	Proverbs 13:14-15:33
Week 19	Dec 28 – Jan 3	1 John 2:28-4:21	Week 46	Jul 5 – Jul 11	1 Thessalonians 1:1-3:13
Week 20	Jan 4 – Jan 10	1 John 5:1 - 3 John 14	Week 47	Jul 12 – Jul 18	1 Thessalonians 4:1-5:28
Week 21	Jan 11 – Jan 17	Ezra 1:1-5:5	Week 48	Jul 19 – Jul 25	2 Thessalonians 1:1-3:18
Week 22	Jan 18 – Jan 24	Ezra 5:6-8:36	Week 49	Jul 26 – Aug 1	Colossians 1:1-2:15
Week 23	Jan 25 – Jan 31	Ezra 9:1 - Haggai 2:23	Week 50	Aug 2 – Aug 8	Colossians 2:16-4:18
Week 24	Feb 1 – Feb 7	Nehemiah 1:1-4:23	Week 51	Aug 9 – Aug 15	2 Peter 1:1-2:22
Week 25	Feb 8 – Feb 14	Nehemiah 5:1-13:14	Week 52	Aug 16 – Aug 22	2 Peter 3:1 - Jude 25
Week 26	Feb 15 – Feb 21	Acts 1:1-3:11	Week 53	Aug 23 – Aug 29	Ruth 1:1-4:22
Week 27	Feb 22 – Feb 28	Acts 3:12-5:32			